Greenock
in old picture postcards

by John Fyfe Anderson, B.A., B.D.

European Library ZALTBOMMEL / THE NETHERLANDS

Bibliography:
Anderson, M. and Monteith J., *Greenock from old photographs,* Inverclyde District Libraries, 1980.
Blair, G., *Greenock Street Names,* Greenock Herald, 1907.
Davies, K., *The Clyde Passenger Steamers,* Kyle Publications, Ayr. 1980.
Dow, J.L., *Greenock,* Greenock Corporation, 1975.
Groome, F.H., *Ordnance Gazetteer of Scotland,* Vol. III, Edinburgh 1883.
McCrorie, I. and Monteith, J., *Clyde Piers,* Inverclyde District Libraries, 1982.
Macdougall, S., *Profiles from the Past,* Inverclyde District Libraries, 1982.
Macdougall, S. and Skee, M., *The Greenock Blitz,* Inverclyde District Libraries, 1991.
Monteith J. and McCarroll, J., *Greenock from old photographs,* Vol. 2, Inverclyde District Libraries, 1983.
Paterson, A.J.S., *The Golden Years of the Clyde Steamers (1889-1914),* David and Charles, Newton Abbot, 1969.
Smith, R.M., *History of Greenock,* Orr, Pollock and Co. Greenock. 1921.
Walker, F.A., *The South Clyde Estuary,* Edinburgh, 1986.
Views and Reminiscences of Old Greenock, James McKelvie and Sons, 1891.
Files of the Greenock Telegraph.
Greenock Directories.
The Statistical Accounts of Scotland: Town and Parish of Greenock, 1793; Parish of Greenock 1836-42; Parish and Burgh of Greenock, 1962.

By the same author:
Bishopton and Langbank in old picture postcards, volumes 1 and 2
Renfrew in old picture postcards
Kilbarchan in old picture postcards
Johnstone in old picture postcards

GB ISBN 90 288 5963 2
© 1994 European Library – Zaltbommel/The Netherlands
Second edition, 1998: reprint of the original edition of 1994.

INTRODUCTION

The town of Greenock is situated on the south bank of the River Clyde 22 ½ miles north-west of the city of Glasgow. The origin of the name of the town is thought to derive from the Gaelic 'grianaig', which means 'sunny'. This has also been translated as 'sunny place' or 'sunny knoll'. The population of Greenock was estimated to be 57,643 in 1992.

It is thought that the original village of Greenock grew up round the religious establishment which gave its name to the Bay of St. Lawrence. This was the chapel of St. Lawrence which was situated at the west corner of Virginia Street, and of which traces remained until 1760. The castle of Wester Greenock was formerly located on the site of Well Park and was the residence of the Shaw family, who exerted considerable influence on the development of the town. The Shaw family have a long connection with Greenock. In 1635 John Shaw obtained a charter from King Charles I which conferred upon Greenock the rights and privileges of a burgh of barony. Until 1741 the burghal affairs of Greenock were superintended by the laird, the feudal superior or by a baron-baillie appointed by him. As a result of a charter dated 30th January 1741 and another in the year 1751, Sir John Shaw gave power to the feuars and sub-feuars to meet annually for the purpose of choosing nine feuars residing in the town to be managers of the burgh funds.

The municipal government and jurisdiction of the town continued to be administered under the charter of 1751 until the Burgh Reform Act of 1833. As a result of that Act the Town Council began to consist of a provost, four bailies, a treasurer and ten councillors. Greenock continued to exist as a burgh until 1975, when the last provost demitted office as a result of the reorganisation of local government in that year, when Greenock became part of the District of Inverclyde within Strathclyde region.

Shipbuilding in Greenock was formerly of great importance. In 1764 the first square-rigged vessel was built by Peter Love. This vessel was appropriately named the 'Greenock'. In 1840 a total of 21 vessels were built with a total tonnage of 7,338 tons. This figure had increased to 20,000 tons by 1876 and 52,744 tons by 1882. In 1958 Greenock yards built nine ships of a total gross tonnage of 60,015 tons.

During the years from 1875 to 1914 there was considerable development of the shipbuilding industry in Greenock. The industry was affected by the depression after the First World War. Those prominent in shipbuilding include John Wood (1788-1860), John Denholm (1853-1937), Sir James Lithgow (1883-1952), and John Scott (1830-1903). The development of Greenock as a port can be seen by the fact that the total tonnage of sailing vessels registered as belonging to Greenock increased from 29,054 tons in 1825 to 168,644 tons in 1881. The total tonnage of steamers rose from 2,012 tons in 1853 to 50,572 tons in 1881.

By the early 1880s a wide range of manufacturing outlets had been established in the town. There were in Greenock and neighbourhood sail-cloth factories, sail-making establishments, ropeworks, woollen factories, a flax mill and a paper mill. There were also sawmills, grain mills, a large cooper work, a distillery, breweries, soap and candle works, a pottery, a straw hat manufacturer and chemical works.

For a considerable period the people of Greenock were almost totally involved in the promotion of industry and commerce to the exclusion of literature and science. This is evident in the case of the poet John Wilson, who was appointed as master of the grammar school of Greenock in 1769, a condition of his employment being that he should abandon 'the profane and unprofitable art of poem-making'. The first book was not printed in the town until 1810, this being undertaken by William Scott. John Mennons began the printing of books in 1821.

The 'Greenock Advertiser' was the first newspaper to be published in the town, this event occuring in 1802. The 'Greenock Herald' commenced publication in 1852. The 'Greenock Telegraph', founded in 1857, continues to be published at the present time. This newspaper was the first halfpenny evening daily paper in Britain. On a further literary note Greenock has associations with the poet and novelist Patrick McGill (1890-1960) and the novelists John Galt (1779-1839) and George Blake (1893-1961).

Undoubtedly James Watt is Greenock's most famous son. He invented the separate condenser for the steam-engine in 1765. He was granted the patent for a 'New method of Lessening the Consumption of Steam and Fuel in Fire Engines' in 1769. James Watt was responsible for carrying out improvements to Greenock Harbour in 1772. His name is commemorated throughout the town in a variety of ways and is also perpetuated in the scientific world by the fact that the unit of power called the 'watt' is named after him.

A large number of prominent individuals have been associated with Greenock. George Burns (1795-1890) of G. and J. Burns, was responsible for establishing the town as the main port of embarkation for sending mail to Ireland. Neil Dougall, who was born in Greenock in 1776 and died in 1862, is mainly remembered for his musical arrangements for the Scottish Metrical Psalms and Paraphrases. William Quarrier, born in the town in 1829, founded the Orphan Homes of Scotland which were in operation near Bridge of Weir from 1878. The artist Patrick Downie (1854-1945) was the first Greenock man who had a painting which was exhibited at the Royal Academy. John Caird (1820-1898) was Professor of Divinity at the University of Glasgow from 1826 to 1873. He was appointed as Principal and Vice Chancellor of the University of Glasgow in 1873 and occupied this position until 1898. His brother, Edward Caird (1835-1908), was also a distinguished academic. He was Professor of Moral Philosophy at the University of Glasgow from 1866 to 1893 and Master of Balliol College, Oxford, from 1893 to 1907. The Caird brothers were the sons of blacksmith John Caird, who was one of the founding partners of the shipbuilding firm of Anderson, Caird and Company.

There are many buildings of architectural interest to be seen in the town. These include the Municipal Buildings, the Sheriff Court, the Custom House, the Watt Monument Library, the mansions of the West End and a large number of churches. Regarding this latter point, the diversity of religious opinion within Greenock was evident by the fact that in 1883 there were thirty-eight places of worship within its boundaries. These belonged to eleven denominations which included the Church of Scotland, the Free Church of Scotland, the United Presbyterian Church, the Roman Catholic Church and the Episcopal Church.

Greenock has changed considerably over the years and its importance as a seaport has declined. Steamers no longer call at the now-demolished Prince's Pier. However, the town has gained a modern image with the building of the present town centre in the 1960s and 1970s. Links with the past have not been forgotten and the residential West End of the town has been designated as an Outstanding Conservation Area. There is also a Conservation Area which is located in the area of William Street and Cathcart Square. Greenock has played an important part in the history of the nation in times of peace and war. Many aspects of the life and history of the town are to be found in the illustrations which are contained in this volume.

Brougham Street, Greenock

1. BROUGHAM STREET. Only horse-drawn traffic is visible in this scene from the beginning of this century. The tram-lines can be seen in the centre of the street with the power-lines overhead suspended from the large standards. Three young children can be seen standing out in the street, which is an indication of the lack of traffic at that period. This street is named after Henry Peter Brougham (1778-1868), 1st Baron Brougham and Vaux. He was educated at Edinburgh High School and the University of Edinburgh, being called to the Scottish Bar in 1800. He later became a well-known advocate and gained distinction as a result of his great speeches. In 1802 he helped to found the 'Edinburgh Review' and contributed extensively to its early issues. He was called to the English Bar in 1812. Henry Brougham became a Member of Parliament in 1830 and was Lord Chancellor from 1830 to 1834. Lord Brougham was the author of 'Historical Sketches of Statesmen who Flourished in the Time of George III'. He was also involved in the founding of the University of London.

BROUGHAM STREET, GREENOCK

2. BROUGHAM STREET. The tram-lines have been removed in this view and re-surfacing has taken place. A bus proceeds along the street, where formerly there were trams. The Greenock Tramway Company was a subsidiary of the Scottish General Transport Company, whose policy was to develop bus services to feed the tramcar system. The tramway company in Greenock which was later renamed Greenock Motor Services, began using buses in 1924 and continued to do so until 1949, when local services were absorbed within the Western S.M.T. Company. In this view there is a request stop sign for Greenock Motor Services attached to the lamp-standard which can be seen near the child on the right, who is pushing a hand-cart. When this scene was photographed there was still little traffic at this location and there were no parked cars lining the street.

3. FINNART STREET. This tree-lined street in the west end of Greenock derives its name from the farm of Finnart. This farm was in the possession of the Shaw Stewart family in former times. It is thought that the name of this street is derived from the Gaelic meaning 'the white point'. The first recorded mention of the lands of Finnart was in 1527, when James Stewart of Ardgowan obtained a precept from Sir James Hamilton of Finnart investing him with certain lands. Sir James' father was the Earl of Arran, who was Lord High Treasurer of Scotland during the reign of King James V. In 1540 Alexander Schaw obtained a charter of the lands of Finnart from the same monarch. This is a view of the street in the 1900s.

Forsyth Street, Greenock.

4. FORSYTH STREET. This street has retained its original character throughout this century. The majority of the trees are still in position. The only person to be seen in this view is the woman with the pram on the right of the street. It can be seen that the street is completely free of traffic, providing a marked contrast to the present time. This street was named after William Forsyth, who was a merchant in Greenock. His house, named 'Rosebank', was erected in the early 1800s at the north-east corner of Union Street. The site on which 'Rosebank' was built, was granted to William Forsyth by Sir John Shaw Stewart for the sum of twelve hundred and sixty-nine pounds, six shillings and eightpence. The feu contract entered into between the aforesaid persons was dated 18th October 1805. A short time after this period, William Forsyth moved to Liverpool. The novelist George Blake was born in the house which is now number 84 Forsyth Street. His best known novel is 'The Shipbuilders', which was published in 1935.

Eldon Street, Greenock.

5. ELDON STREET. This scene has changed as a result of the removal of the tram-lines and the large standards which carried the power-ones. This street was named after John Scott, 1st Earl of Eldon (1751-1838). He was a lawyer and politician who was born in Newcastle. He became a Member of Parliament in 1782, was appointed as Solicitor-General in 1788 and Attorney-General in 1793. He was appointed as Lord Chancellor in 1801. Lord Eldon was opposed to reform and religious liberty. It was in the latter issue that he had a particular association with Greenock. This was in connection with the proposed Catholic Emancipation Bill in 1829, when he received nine hundred petitions against the Bill from various parts of the country. Amongst these, there was one from Greenock and in presenting it to the House of Commons, he remarked 'that this was a proof of education in Scotland, and in particular in Greenock, that in a petition so numerously signed (five thousand names) the signatures were all written and only three marks'.

6. ELDON STREET. This substantial mansion in the West End of the town has been demolished. The site of this property is now occupied by the recently constructed buildings of MacLehose Court. This postcard was originally sent to Limoges, France. The sender's home was at 9 Eldon Street.

7. CATHCART STREET. An open-topped tram proceeds along Cathcart Street in this view. From 1871 until 1929 a limited tram service operated in the town. The trams were horse-drawn until electrification took place in 1898. In the first instance the trams operated in Greenock and Gourock, but in 1889 the service was extended to Port Glasgow. Originally a complete network of tramway routes was projected in Greenock, but the steeper parts of the town prevented such a expansion.

Greenock, Cathcart Street.

8. CATHCART STREET. Horse-drawn traffic proceeds along Cathcart Street in this view from the early years of this century. The buildings on the immediate right have been demolished and replaced by new shop and business premises. The Post Office is the building second from the right of this view. It was built in 1898-1899 and has a Renaissance façade. Here it can be seen that there are two entrances to the Post Office. Now, only the entrance on the left is used. It is surmounted by a sculptured head of Queen Victoria. The other entrance has been closed and the sculptured head of Prince Albert has been replaced by a clock. The steeple of the Mid Kirk acts as a focal point in this view. The first congregation of this church was formed in 1741 and worshipped in a nearby loft until this building was completed in 1761. The design of the church was inspired by St. Martin's-in-the-Fields in London. It comprises a square hall, galleried on three sides with ornamental pillars, supporting a pavilion roof, and an internal sweeping coved cornice. The steeple was added in 1787 and is 146 ft in height. This church was refurbished in 1878 and a suite of halls was added in 1936.

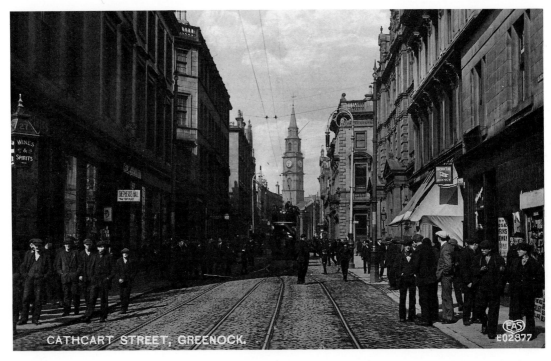

CATHCART STREET, GREENOCK.

E02877

9. CATHCART STREET. The steeple of the Mid Kirk acts as a focal point in this view. On the right of the street there is a sign for an agency for the Anchor Line which operated transatlantic sailings. Cathcart Street also has another connection with shipping. It was at No. 41 Cathcart Street, where John Denholm (1853-1937) opened a factor's office in 1866. As a result of his success in the property business he was able to further his interest in shipping, and established connections with shipowners in Liverpool, London, Bristol Channel ports and Glasgow. In 1869 John Denholm joined with his brother James to found the firm of J. and J. Denholm Ltd. By the beginning of this century the firm owned six steamers in single ship companies. John Denholm was a past President of the Chamber of Shipping of the U.K. and of the Baltic and International Maritime Conference. He also held office as Provost of Greenock from 1904 to 1909 and was a former Chairman of the town's Harbour Board. In addition, he held office as Norwegian Consul at Greenock. John Denholm was awarded the honour of Knight Bachelor of the Royal Order of St. Olav, First Class, in 1929.

HAMILTON STREET, GREENOCK.

10. HAMILTON STREET. This scene has completely changed and is now known as Hamilton Way. The buildings on both sides of the street have been demolished. New shops have been built and the area has been pedestrianised. In 1765 the Town Council built a Town House in Hamilton Street on the site of the present Municipal Buildings. Cathcart Street and Hamilton Street were each in turn referred to as the High Street. An old house in Hamilton Street which was demolished over 170 years ago bore the date 1769 on its crow-stepped gable. Older dates were found on nearby properties at that time.

11. HAMILTON STREET. A section of the Municipal Buildings can be seen on the right of this view. All of the builings on the left have been demolished and this site, including part of Hamilton Street, was laid out as Clyde Square in 1975. This plan was first suggested in the 1940s. The imposing lamp posts outside the Municipal Buildings have been removed as has the large lamp standard on the left. The Municipal Buildings were built in the years 1879-1886, the architects being Messrs. H. and D. Barclay of Glasgow. The decision to proceed with the erection of the Municipal Buildings took place at a special meeting of the Town Council in August 1877. In September 1879 over eighty designs were submitted for the proposed buildings. The foundation stone, which was located in one of the piers of the Victoria Tower, was laid on 6th August 1891 by Provost Dugald Campbell. The site of the Municipal Buildings cost £ 58,000 and it was estimated that the construction work would be £ 80,000. The final cost was about £ 200,000.

WEST BLACKHALL STREET, GREENOCK

12. WEST BLACKHALL STREET. Pedestrians of differing ages stand in both the centre and side of the street, which is an indication of the lack of traffic in the early years of this century. The cobbled surface in this street has been retained, but as elsewhere in Greenock the tram lines have been removed. Two buildings of interest in this street are the tenement blocks of Lorne Court and 77-93 West Blackhall Street. At No. 131 there is Grey Place House, which was built about 1840. It is rubble-built and also has two of the attic dormers which are a feature of Greenock buildings.

WEST BLACKHALL STREET, GREENOCK.

13. WEST BLACKHALL STREET. A prominent sign indicating the premises of Hodge's at 12 and 14 West Blackhall Street can be seen on the right of this view. The full name of this business was Hodge, Mitchell and Son. This firm were cabinetmakers, upholsterers, bedding manufacturers and complete house-furnishers. Leather goods, prams and toys were also sold in these premises. Hodge's also undertook carpet-beating and removals. The firm also had premises in the Municipal Buildings, Hamilton Street. There were also branches of Hodge's at 38 Church Street, Port Glasgow and 67 Kempock Street, Gourock. The firm is no longer in business at these premises in West Blackhall Street. A further point regarding this street is that the cobblestone surface remains. However, the tram-lines and overhead wires have been removed.

West Blackhall Street, Greenock.

14. WEST BLACKHALL STREET. A variety of horse-drawn traffic can be seen in this view of West Blackhall Street in the early years of this century. Horses were formerly not only used widely to pull carts and wagons, but also in other ways. An example of this was in the sugar stores of Messrs. Gray and Buchanan, which were located at the north-west corner of Argyle Street and West Blackhall Street. In the middle of last century casks of sugar were hoisted into the lofts of these premises by means of horse haulage. In order to reach the higher floors of the warehouse it was necessary for the horses to traverse the entire breadth of the street. This method of hoisting goods was also used in the other parts of the town. However, the practice later became quite unsuitable in busy thoroughfares such as West Blackhall Street, and finally ceased as a result of the adoption of the hydraulic hoist. In about 1870 Messrs. Gray and Buchanan sold their warehouse in West Blackhall Street to Thomas Suttie, who converted it into shops and offices.

MORTON TERRACE, GREENOCK

15. MORTON TERRACE. Morton Terrace is now known as Carwood Street. A number of changes have taken place in this street as the trees and lamp-posts have been removed, the cobblestone surface no longer remains and the chimney-heads at the front of the tenements have been removed. No traffic whatsoever is to be seen in this view which is in marked contrast to the present time. These tenements, built about 1875, are located in the eastern suburb of Cartsdyke. It was also known as Crawfurdsdyke. Cartsdyke became a burgh of barony in 1636, and at one time it was regarded as being more important than.Greenock itself . In 1696 one of the ships for the ill-fated Darien Expedition was fitted out there. Cartsdyke was also well-known for the curing of red herring. It remained a distinct community until its merger with Greenock in 1841.

MORTON SQUARE, GREENOCK.

16. MORTON SQUARE. This view shows Carwood Street, Cartsdyke, from the opposite direction to the previous illustration. In this peaceful scene from the 1900s a horse and cart can be seen, while a woman with a pram poses for the camera with her child in the middle of the street. The house at the far end of the street has been demolished and the lamp-post mounted on the plinth has been removed. Cartsdyke was originally a burgh and was granted a charter in 1669. The Crawfurds of Cartsburn in Cartsdyke were the most important family in this community and it was round their mansion that this former burgh grew and developed. Cartsdyke suffered from severe floods in March 1815 and November 1835. On both occasions there was considerable damage to property while in the flood which occurred in 1835 thirty-seven people lost their lives. At a later period during the Greenock Blitz of May 1941 much of Victorian Cartsdyke was destroyed by enemy action and as a consequence many new buildings have been erected.

Greenock Esplanade

17. GREENOCK ESPLANADE. A donkey and cart stands alone in the Esplanade which is devoid of other traffic. The Esplanade was built by the Harbour Trust according to a plan drawn up by Bell and Miller, civil engineers from Glasgow. Work on this project commenced in 1863 and was completed in 1876 at a cost of £ 18,428. The original estimate for the project had been £ 12,000. Provost Robert Neill was critical of the amount spent on the Esplanade considering the finances which were then available to the Town Council at that time. Soil which was excavated during the building of the Albert Harbour was used in the construction of the foundation of the Esplanade. On the Esplanade there is a fountain which has been erected in memory of the novelist John Galt (1779-1839) who resided in Greenock from 1790 to 1804 and from 1834 until his death. There is also a buoy in position on the Esplanade. It was originally laid down by the Trustees of the Clyde Lighthouses Trust at Rosneath Point in 1880 and was the first flashing buoy to be set up in order to aid navigation. Henry Robertson Bowers (1883-1911), who was born in Greenock, is commemorated by a plaque which is located in the Esplanade near North Street. He was a member of Captain Scott's expedition to the South Pole during 1910-1912.

Esplanade, Greenock.

18. ESPLANADE. A paddle-steamer sails up-river past the west end of the Esplanade in this scene, which was a very common occurrence in past years. In this view two seated figures and one on the roof of the boat clubhouse have their gaze directed towards the river, while a group of boys pose for the photographer near the fountain, which has since been removed. The Esplanade at Greenock is considered to be one of the finest of its type ever constructed in the West of Scotland.

Princes Pier, Greenock,
with G. & S.W. Ry. Co's. Steamer "Neptune".

19. 'NEPTUNE', PRINCE'S PIER. The 'Neptune' was built in 1892 by Napier, Shanks and Bell Ltd. of Glasgow and had a accommodation for 1,267 passengers. The cost of her construction amounted to £19,164. The Glasgow and South Western Railway Company had the 'Neptune' built as a sister ship to the 'Mercury' for their Lower Clyde railway connections and cruises. The 'Neptune' was launched on 10th March 1892 and had her trials eighteen days later when she achieved a speed of 18 knots. This was more than the guaranteed speed of 17.45 knots and as a result the 'Neptune' was regarded as the fastest paddle-steamer of her length afloat. On 31st March 1892 she went on an inaugural trip from Prince's Pier to the Kyles of Bute with a party of guests of the directors of the Company and Napier, Shanks and Bell Ltd. The 'Neptune' had very comfortable passenger accommodation. Part of the Glasgow Herald's description of the vessel is as follows: 'The first class dining saloon, which is seated for seventy and is situated below the general saloon, is furnished pretty much in the style of the drawing room. The ceilings and sides are beautifully decorated and the floors laid with tastefully designed carpets and runners. On each side of the central passage are handsome mahogany tables, while right around the saloon run velvet-cushioned seats.'

Greenock from the Harbour.

RELIABLE SERIES. 0218

20. GREENOCK FROM THE HARBOUR. In the closing years of the seventeenth century repeated efforts were made by Sir John Shaw and his son to obtain parliamentary powers and assistance to extend the harbour accommodation of the port and to levy dues to cover this expense. On three occasions these efforts were defeated by the resistance of the royal burghs on the Clyde in combination with burghs all over Scotland. However, Sir John Shaw's son, also called Sir John, advanced the sum of £ 5,000 in order to construct the new harbour. This money was advanced by Sir John on condition that he should be repaid by a levy of almost 7p on every sack of malt brewed into ale within the burgh. This debt was cleared within thirty years. The work on the new project began in 1707, with gardeners and masons being brought from Edinburgh to assist in the construction work.

21. PRINCE'S PIER. The building of this pier began in 1862 and was completed in 1870 at a cost of almost £ 100,000. Prince's Pier was mainly used as a port-of-call for railway and river steamers. The original frontage extended to 2,206 feet, of which the sea frontage for deep-sea steamers consisted of 1,250 feet. The remaining part of the pier was an enclosed boat harbour. Prince's Pier was built out into the former Bay of Quick. It was connected by rail to St. Enoch's Station in Glasgow and was formerly one of the busiest piers on the Clyde. The number of steamers which used this pier began to decline as early as the 1920s. However, during the Second World War the pier was rebuilt in order to serve as one of the terminals for troop transport. The passenger train service to Prince's Pier was terminated in January 1959. The station was still used after that time to convey passengers from Glasgow for the transatlantic liners which called at the Tail o' the Bank, this traffic having now completely ceased. The station buildings on Prince's Pier have been demolished and replaced by the Clydeport Container Terminal, which was opened in 1969.

22. PRINCE'S PIER. The vessel on the right is the 'Minerva'. She was built in 1893 by J. and G. Thomson of Clydebank and launched on 6th May of that year. The 'Minerva' weighed 306 tons and could carry 1,035 passengers. This vessel was one of the fleet of steamers owned by the Glasgow and South Western Railway Company. She was specially-designed not only for service in winter, but also for summer excursions in the outer waters of the Firth of Clyde. Twice in 1894 the 'Minerva' was involved in two incidents with the 'Galatea', which was owned by the Caledonian Steam Packet Company. The second of these resulted in a collision between these vessels at Kirn pier. At the trial which later took place in the Marine Police Court, Glasgow, the master of 'Miverva' was declared innocent, while Captain Duncan Bell of the 'Galatea' was convicted. During the First World War the 'Minerva' was converted for minesweeping duties, but she was captured by the Turks in 1917. After the conclusion of hostilities she was sold by the Turks for service as a Bosphorus ferry. It is thought that this vessel was broken up in 1929.

Greenock, Princes Pier

23. PRINCE'S PIER. The station buildings shown on the left of this view were formally opened on 25th May 1894. On that day a special train conveyed officers of the Glasgow and South Western Railway Company and guests along with representatives from the Press. It left from St. Enoch's Station for Prince's Pier. On arrival there, the party inspected the new station and pier buildings and afterwards went on a cruise to Loch Striven in the 'Neptune'. These buildings replaced the former station, which had originally been built by the Greenock and Ayrshire Railway Company in 1869. The new station was of much larger dimensions than the previous one had been. The Italianate towers were a dominating feature in the wide façade, which was built of red Ruabon brick. The platforms of the station protected by verandah roofs were above pier level and at right angles to it. Two carriage ways, two flights of stairs and two luggage lifts connected upper and lower levels of the building. The Marine Superintendent, Captain Duncan Williamson, his staff and railway officials had accommodation in the upper part of the buildings.

Princes Pier, Greenock.

24. PRINCE'S PIER. The paddle steamer 'Mercury' berths at Prince's Pier in the mid-1930s. This vessel was built in 1934 by the Fairfield Engineering Co. Ltd. of Govan for the London Midland and Scottish Railway. She weighed 621 tons, had a speed of 17 ½ knots and could carry 1,892 passengers. One of the features of the 'Mercury' was that she had disguised paddle-boxes which resulted in some criticism. She began service on the Greenock to Kyles of Bute run. Early in the Second World War the 'Mercury' was requisitioned by the Admiralty and was converted for use as a minesweeper. She initially served with the 1st Minesweeping Flotilla, which worked from the Clyde to the Irish coast. At a later period she served with the 11th Minesweeping Flotilla, which was based at Milford Haven in Pembrokeshire. However, while serving with this flotilla, the 'Mercury' was struck by a mine off the Irish Coast on Christmas Eve 1940. As a result of this she sank, but all on board were saved. There was also a previous paddle steamer called the 'Mercury'. She was built in 1892 and was broken up in 1933. She was built by Napier, Shanks and Bell and was owned by the Glasgow and South Western Railway.

LYNDOCH ST GREENOCK.

25. LYNEDOCH STREET. This is a view of Lynedoch Street looking towards the entrance to the Well Park in Regent Street. The tenements on the right have been demolished while those on the left remain in position. This street is named after Thomas Graham, 1st Baron Lynedoch, who was born in 1748. His father was the Laird of Balgowan in Perthshire. In 1774 he married Lady Mary, second daughter of the ninth Lord Cathcart, and this appears to be the main connection which he had with Greenock. He followed a military career and in 1794 he raised the 90th Regiment of Foot (the Perthshire Regiment) later serving with it as its Colonel in Minorca in 1798. In 1809 Colonel Graham was aide-de-camp to General Sir John Moore at Corunna. He also participated in many other military actions during the Peninsular War of 1808-1814. In 1814 he was created as Baron Lynedoch of Balgowan. Three years later he founded the Senior United Service Club. Lord Lynedoch also previously served as a Member of Parliament in addition to his military duties. He was first elected as M.P. for Perthshire in 1794 and was returned unopposed in the General Elections of 1796 and 1802, resigning as an M.P. in 1807. Lord Lynedoch died in his 96th year.

GLENVIEW TERRACE, GREENOCK.

26. GLENVIEW TERRACE. The well-built terraced houses in Glenview Terrace remain substantially unaltered in this view from 1919. Here a 'For Sale' notice is displayed above the entrance to the second house on the left. The lamp-posts have been removed, but the road and pavement surfaces have been improved since that time. A small block of shops was built on the left of this view in what is now Murdieston Street. The trees on the right have been removed and there are now houses on that site. The gable-ends of the tenements in the distance are also in Murdieston Street.

NEWARK STREET, GREENOCK.

27. NEWARK STREET. In this scene there are the lines of trees which are a feature of the West End of the town. Here the dense foliage of the trees obscure the houses in the middle distance and also Finnart St. Paul's Church. Part of the section of terraced houses can be seen on the right of this view. These are contained within the terraced houses from Nos. 38-50 Newark Street. The total absence of traffic in this wide street evokes a tranquillity which is not to be found in the present day as a result of increased traffic. At number 12 Newark Street there is a towered Italianate mansion, which was built circa 1860. A house in the Elizabehan style, known as Madeira Lodge, is located at 16 Newark Street. It was built in about 1840. Greenock Academy is now located to the left of this view, the main entrance being in Madeira Street. This school was built in 1964 by Burnet, Bell and Partners.

NEWARK STREET FROM UNION STREET, GREENOCK.

67927 JV

28. NEWARK STREET. The property on the right is Nos. 8-10 Newark Street. The feuing plan in 1818 for the West End of the town was the commencement of an undertaking, the purpose of which was to design a new town of a considerable extent. A number of streets were marked and named, from the West Burn to the Battery on the west, southward to the foot of the Whinhill, and up to Hillend in the Carts-dyke district. In 1818 there were only about twenty properties in what is now the West End. Despite the slow progress of development in this area, Daniel Weir in his 'History of Greenock' written in 1829, stated that by this time the town, although having a rather irregular appearance, contained many excellent buildings. The town was also expanding westwards and there had been rapid progress in the lay-ing-out of new streets. In addition, a number of fine villas were scattered from east to west and also along the shore.

Demolition of Roxburgh Sugar Refinery Chimney, Greenock, by David Tosh & Son, 8th April, 1909.

29. DEMOLITION OF ROXBURGH SUGAR REFINERY CHIMNEY. The demolition of this 160 ft chimney was observed by thousands of spectators. Between 10 and 11 a.m. on 8th April 1909 crowds of people gathered in the vicinity of the chimney, but in Roxburgh Street and Holmscroft Street police were stationed to keep them at a safe distance from the scene of operations. Spectators also lined the slopes at Prospecthill. By 11.15 a.m. everything was in readiness, and when the explosive charges were set off, the chimney crashed down into the grounds of the refinery towards Duncan Street. A reporter from the 'Greenock Telegraph' wrote as follows: 'It was a nerve-stirring scene, and relief was felt when the whole affair had passed off without any mishap.' A further report in the same newspaper reads as follows: 'From Duncan Street we had an uninterrupted view. It was a wonderful scene, but many of us wished we hadn't got so near when the charge went off and the stalk came moving towards us. Yet it was a sight not to be missed.' The contract for the demolition of the chimney was given to the Greenock firm of David Tosh and Son because of their expertise in this type of work.

Charing Cross, showing
Messrs. Scott's Main shipbuilding Yard, Greenock

GORDON.

30. CHARING CROSS. The premises of Scott's Shipbuilding and Engineering Co. Ltd. can be seen on the left of this view. This company was founded in 1711 by John Scott, who built herring busses and smaller boats in a yard at the mouth of the West Burn, on ground which was leased from Sir John Shaw. Later in the eighteenth century Scott's began to build large steam-going vessels. In 1787-1789 large plots of ground were purchased from Lord Cathcart in order to build extensions to the existing shipbuilding yard. This resulted in the firm almost entirely occupying the foreshore from the West Quay to the West Burn. By 1816 Scott's had built two of the earliest Clyde steamers, these being the 'Active' and the 'Despatch'. This firm also had the distinction of having built the first steam frigate from a Clyde shipbuilding yard for the Royal Navy. This vessel was the H.M.S. 'Greenock', which was launched in 1849. She was the largest iron warship of her time and was the first to be fitted by Scott's with the screw propeller. John Scott (1830-1903) and his brother Robert Sinclair Scott were responsible for significant progress in the firm. The brothers totally reconstructed the Cartsdyke shipyard, which had originally been acquired in 1850. They also purchased the shipbuilding yard and drydock of Roger Steele and Sons and it was there that they established the Cartsburn Yard.

WELLPARK AND WAR MEMORIAL. GREENOCK

31. WELL PARK AND WAR MEMORIAL. This memorial was unveiled in the Well Park on 4th October 1924, when a total of 20,000 people were present to witness the ceremony, which took place in bright autumn sunshine. The official proceedings commenced with the band of the 171st Heavy Battery Royal Artillery, who played Carlon's 'Voluntary Andante Religioso', followed by the singing of the 23rd Psalm. The unveiling ceremony was performed by Mrs. John Forbes, five of whose sons lost their lives in the First World War. Then the memorial was dedicated by the Rev. W.J. Nichol Service, who was then minister of the West Parish Church, Greenock. He offered prayers for all of the men from Greenock who had been killed in the First World War. One minute's silence followed the conclusion of this prayer. The silence was broken by the sounding of the Last Post by the trumpeters of the 77th Highland Field Brigade Royal Artillery and the 'Flowers of the Forest' played by the pipe band of the Argyll and Sutherland Highlanders. Sir Hugh Shaw Stewart, Lord Lieutenant of Renfrewshire, then made a moving tribute to the men of Greenock who had died in the war.

32. WAR MEMORIAL. This shows a close-up of the Greenock War Memorial. The winged figure of Victory similar to the figurehead borne on the prow of ancient Greek galleys of war is a reminder of those who served in the Navy. The representation of the two-handed sword on the Celtic cross is a tribute to those who joined the Army and particularly to those who served in Scottish regiments. Many regiments are represented in the roll of those who died, but the most prominent is that of the 400 men of the Argyll and Sutherland Highlanders who lost their lives in the First World War. The architects for the memorial were Messrs. Wright and Wylie. The sculptor was Alexander Proudfoot, while the contractors for the obelisk were Messrs. Matthew Muir and Co. Dr. Pittendreigh MacGillivray, the King's Sculptor in Scotland, and Mr. G. Washington Browne, President of the Royal Scottish Academy, also provided guidance in the design of this structure to the Citizens' War Memorial Committee, who were entrusted with the erection of this memorial. The 'Greenock Telegraph' of 6th October 1924 described the memorial as 'a chaste and dignified structure, a living and enduring memorial to the men of Greenock who fell in the Great War'.

33. WATT MONUMENT. This monument is located in Greenock Cemetery and consists of a wide variety of stones from all over the world. A stone from St. Paul's Bay, Malta, was donated by a former Governor of the Island, Sir William Reid. Marble from Tunis was donated by Sir Edward Baines and also by Admiral Sir Houston Stewart. Other stones include a slab from Palestine, a stone from Peru and red sandstone from Seneca Quarry, Potomac River, Maryland, USA. There is also a pentagonal column from the Giant's Causeway in Northern Ireland. Stones were also presented by the Bombay Mechanics' Institution and the Mechanics' Institute, St. Helenstone, Canada. It was in 1854 when the Watt Club decided to erect a tower in memory of James Watt. It was originally planned that the monument should be a massive 189 feet in height. The cairn was not completed until 1936, which was the 200th anniversary of Watt's birth.

King's Theatre and Hippodrome, Greenock

34. KING'S THEATRE AND HIPPODROME. The King's Theatre is the domed building on the left of this view. It was originally known as the Alexandra Theatre, the building having been constructed in 1905 at the corner of Ker Street and Grey Place in 1905 with seating accommodation for 1,900. This building became the King's Theatre from 1910. In 1928 the theatre was converted into a cinema with 'talkies' being shown from 1937. During the Second World War some shows were produced for the benefit of servicemen in the area. A further change of ownership occurred in 1955, when the building was purchased by the Rank Organisation and became the Odeon. In 1973 the former King's Theatre was demolished as a result of a compulsory purchase order. The Hippodrome is the taller building to the right of the King's Theatre in this view of West Blackhall Street. It dated from 1858, when it was known as the Theatre Royal. It became the Hippodrome after previously being the Palace Music Hall and the Pavilion. The Hippodrome closed in 1923 and was demolished in 1930.

Photo. by John Walker   Printed by John Mitchell Pollock

35. GREENOCK AMATEUR OPERATIC SOCIETY. This picture shows the cast for the society's production of 'The Pirates of Penzance' in the early 1900s. There is a strong tradition of music in Greenock, which has had a significant impact on the cultural life of the town. The composer Hamish MacCunn was born at 37 Ardgowan Street in 1868. He studied under Sir Hubert Parry at the Royal College of Music, London, from 1883 till 1886. Hamish MacCunn was professor af Harmony at the Royal Academy of Music from 1888 till 1894. He composed the opera 'Jeanie Deans' in 1894 and that of 'Diarmid and Ghrine' in 1899. MacCunn also composed cantatas, orchestral pieces, pieces for violin, piano and cello, and about eighty songs. He is particularly remembered for his romantic overture 'Land of the Mountain and the Flood'. Hamish MacCunn died in 1916.

36. GREENOCK AMATEUR OPERATIC SOCIETY. The large company of the Greenock Operatic Society pose for the camera in a wide variety of costumes and headgear for their roles in the production of Gilbert and Sullivan's 'Yeomen of the Guard' in the early years of this century. Two further composers born in Greenock were Allan Macbeth (1856-1910) and William Wallace (1860-1940). Allan Macbeth was an organist, choral director and composer. He studied at the Leipzig Conservatory. Macbeth was conductor of the Glasgow Choral Union from 1880 until 1887 and was appointed as principal of the music school of the Glasgow Athenaeum in 1890. He also composed piano pieces, orchestral works, cantatas, part-songs and chamber music. William Wallace qualified in medicine before studying at the Royal Academy of Music in London. He composed orchestral and vocal works. He was also the first composer in Britain to write a symphonic poem. This occured in 1892 with his writing of 'The Passing of Beatrice'. William Wallace was the author of the following books: 'The Threshold of Music (1908); 'The Musical Faculty' (1914); 'A Study of Wagner' (1925); and 'Liszt, Wagner and the Princess' (1928).

Belville Street, Greenock

67923

37. BELVILLE STREET. This view shows Belville Street in the years before the First World War. During the Greenock Blitz of 6th-7th May 1941 the tenements at 37 and 43-45 Belville Street were destroyed as a result of bombing by German aircraft. There were some survivors from the tenement at number 37, these people having taken cover in the cellar at that address. In 1960 plans were made by Greenock Corporation to rebuild the Belville Street area. In 1963 St. Kenneth's Primary School was opened and replaced St. Lawrence's School in Belville Street. This school was the first to be built in the east end of the town since the Second World War. This part of Belville Street is now known as Carwood Street.

MACGREGOR.

James Watt Dock showing Entrance Gates, Greenock.

38. JAMES WATT DOCK. On 13th June 1878 the Greenock Harbour trustees made a decision to build a new dock and a contract was given to Mr. John Waddell. The main reasons for building the dock were because of the constantly increasing volume of trade and for making more provision for cargo and passenger steamers. The foundation stone of the James Watt Dock was laid on 6th August 1881, which was the same day on which a similar ceremony took place at the new Municipal Buildings. Five years later, on 5th August 1886, the official opening ceremony of the James Watt Dock took place. The total cost of building the James Watt Dock and the price of the ground amounted to £ 850,000. The first estimated cost of the undertaking was £ 208,000. A report in the 'Greenock Telegraph' described how Greenock for the first time in its history stood forth as one of the greatest and best equipped of British seaports as a result of the construction of the James Watt Dock.

The South End, James Watt Dock, Greenock.

39. THE SOUTH END, JAMES WATT DOCK. The turbine screw steamers 'Queen Alexandra' and 'King Edward' are berthed alongside one another in this view. The 'T.S.S. Queen Alexandra' was built by William Denny and Bros. Ltd. of Dumbarton in 1902. She was able to travel at a speed of 21 knots. The 'Queen Alexandra' was a popular steamer, but her service on the Clyde came to an abrupt end in 1911, when she was badly damaged by fire in the Albert Harbour, Greenock. The amount of damage to the vessel was estimated at £ 3,000-£ 4,000. However, she was refitted after the fire before being sold to the Canadian Pacific Railway, and re-named the 'Princess Patricia'. A second 'T.S.S. Queen Alexandra' was built by William Denny and Bros. Ltd. in 1912. The 'T.S.S. King Edward' was the first commercial turbine passenger steamer in the world. She was owned by the Turbine Syndicate from 1901 till 1902 and Turbine Steamers Ltd. from 1902 to 1927. It was 1927 when she came under the ownership of Williamson Buchanan Steamers Ltd. The 'King Edward' had two further changes of ownership, her final one being with the Caledonian Steam Packet Company. This steamer was broken up at Troon in 1952. During the First World War the 'King Edward' transported troops across the English Channel. Her service in the Second World War was mainly confined to ferry runs in home waters.

40. ANN STREET. This scene in Ann Street has completely changed. The buildings on the left of this view have been demolished and have been replaced by a tower-block. The South Parish Church had also been demolished and its site is now within the ground occupied by Wellington Academy. Ann Street was formerly one of the busiest streets in Greenock and was also one of the steepest. At one time a large area of ground in this locality was leased by Ann Bearhope for use as a market garden. Ann Street and Bearhope Street were named after her. The Rev. Charles Durward was the first minister of the South Parish Church and served here from 1875 until 1881. He was followed by the Rev. John Forbes Macpherson, who was minister from 1881 until 1919 and a former clerk of the Presbytery of Greenock. A stained-glass memorial in his memory was erected in the west window of the church in 1933. The Rev. John Youngson Thomson was minister from 1920 until 1931. The Rev. William Hallam McKerracher became the minister of this church in 1931. During the Second World War he was a Chaplain to the Forces and served in the following locations: France 1939-1940; England 1940-1941; Persia (now Iran) and the Middle East 1941-1945.

Brachelston Square, Greenock.

41. BRACHELSTON SQUARE. This is a view looking from Nelson Street. The lamp-post in the centre has been removed and there is now a roundabout in this location. The absence of vehicles is noticeable and also the three men on the left, who are engaged in conversation while standing in the street on the left of this view. The avenue behind the gates on the right leads to Greenock Cemetery. These gates were designed by Charles Wilson in 1847. One of the important monuments in this cemetery is one in the form of a cairn, which was erected in memory of James Watt. It consists of a wide variety of stones which were sent from many parts of the world, and bearing appropriate inscriptions. The foundation stones of the cairn were donated by Dugald Dove of the Nitshill and Arden Quarries and Sir Michael R. Shaw Stewart, Bart. Within the cemetery there are memorials erected in memory of Robert Wallace, who was M.P. for Greenock from 1833 until 1885, and Walter Baine, M.P. for Greenock from 1845 until 1847 and a former provost of the town. More recently, there is a memorial which was unveiled by Provost Robert Boyd on 6th May 1951, that date being the tenth anniversary of the Greenock Blitz. The inscription on this memorial reads as follows: 'Dedicated to the Everlasting Memory of the Citizens of Greenock Who Died as a Result of the Air Raids 1940-1941.'

42. WEST END. Some of the substantial mansions in the West End of the town can be seen in this view. The large property with the conservatory on the left of this picture was known as Stoneleigh. It was formerly the residence of the shipbuilder Arthur Caird, but was demolished in 1948 by Greenock Corporation, who afterwards built houses at this location. The church in this view is Finnart-St. Paul's which is situated in Newark Street. This church was built in 1893, the architect being R. Rowand Anderson. It was formerly St. Paul's Church before uniting with Finnart Church in 1978. The Rev. Dr. Charles Laing Warr, who was minister of this church from 1918 until 1926, achieved great distinction in the Church of Scotland. He was minister of St. Giles' Cathedral Edinburgh from 1926 to 1962. In addition, he was Dean of the Chapel Royal in Scotland and Dean of the Thistle from 1926 until 1969. Dr. Warr held these three offices for a longer period than any of his predecessors.

43. ARDGOWAN SQUARE. This is a view of Union Street with Ardgowan Square on the left of the picture. There is the rather unusual sight of two men standing on the pavement beside the lamp-post with loads on their heads! The road surface in this scene from the early 1900s is markedly different from that of today. Behind the railings on the left of this view the roof of the club-house of Ardgowan Bowling Club is visible. The houses of Ardgowan Square face towards the bowling green. The square itself is an example of thoughtful urban planning. The church tower seen in the distance is that of St. Andrew's Church, formerly Trinity Church. It was designed by John Starforth in 1871. The name of Ardgowan has strong local connections. The first Ardgowan House, which was the ancient stronghold of the Stewart family, was built against the old tower of Inverkip, which was first granted by King Robert III, who reigned from 1390 until 1406. The present Ardgowan House was designed by Hugh Cairncross for Sir John Shaw Stewart, in the years 1798-1801.

BRISBANE STREET. GREENOCK.

44. BRISBANE STREET. The substantial tenements in Brisbane Street are seen in this view from the early years of the present century. Children can be seen standing in the middle of the traffic-free street, a situation which would not be possible today because of the increase in traffic. A further difference is that there are now large numbers of cars parked along both sides of the street. The lamp-posts have also been removed. Brisbane Street is named after Sir Thomas Macdougall Brisbane (1773-1860). He was the first person to sail from the Clyde with all the necessary instruments for ascertaining his position at sea with any degree of accuracy. Sir Thomas entered the army at 16, and served in Flanders, the West Indies, Spain and North America. In 1813 he was promoted to the rank of Major-General. From 1821 until 1825 he was Governor of New South Wales. While Sir Thomas was in Australia he catalogued a total of 7,385 stars, for which he received the Copley medal from the Royal Society. Brisbane, the capital of Queensland, is named after him.

Radiant Series. Extraordinary Rainfall at Greenock, 14th October. Hamilton Street Looking East. 1916.

45. HAMILTON STREET. A tramcar proceeds along Hamilton Street amidst the extensive flooding which occured on 14th October 1916 due to heavy rainfall. On that morning it had rained steadily but between 2 and 3 p.m. the storm burst over Greenock with considerable force. In the streets gutters were converted into miniature canals and in the West End of the town water flowed down the sloping garden paths. Within a short space of time lakes formed at different points along the main thoroughfares. The water encroached on many of the shops and for a time business was almost at a standstill in the affected areas. Houses in Newton Street were flooded with the water level rising to a height of five feet in some instances. The gardens in the West End of the town suffered considerable damage and great quantities of gravel had accumulated at the bottom of the steep streets which led to Eldon Street due to the force of the water. Similarly, large stones were carried down Bentinck Steet. Many branches were also stripped off the trees and on the morning of 15th October 1916 men were employed in clearing this debris from the streets. The storm abated at about 3 p.m. on 14th October and with the tide receding the water quickly disappeared from the streets of Greenock.

46. SANDRINGHAM TERRACE. This four-storey terrace was built in the years 1900-1901 and is located at 1-12 Esplanade. It is considered to be one of the best designed properties of its period. One of the attractions of these tenements for the former occupants would have been the fine views of the River Clyde with the great variety of vessels which then plied its waters. The writer of this postcard was Alexander Kerr, who was then residing at 8 Sandringham Terrace. In his message on the card he stated the following: 'In front is the river, a perfect panorama.' The theme on the river is continued in the tiles which line the close at 3 Sandringham Terrace, on which are represented scenes from the Clyde such as steamers and yachts.

67922　　　**MARGARET STREET, GREENOCK**　　　VALENTINES SERIES

47. MARGARET STREET. The four-storey red sandstone tenements in Margaret Street are a continuation of Sandringham Terrace. The tiles which line the closes of 4, 8 and 10 Margaret Street incorporate Clyde scenes such as hills, steamers and yachts. These are a particularly interesting architectural feature and their colourful appearance is a tangible reminder of the great importance of the Clyde to Greenock throughout its long history. These tiles were manufactured by J. Duncan Ltd. of Glasgow. This view looking up a deserted Margaret Street evokes a sense of peace and tranquillity in an age when parked cars were not a dominant aspect of residential areas in Greenock.

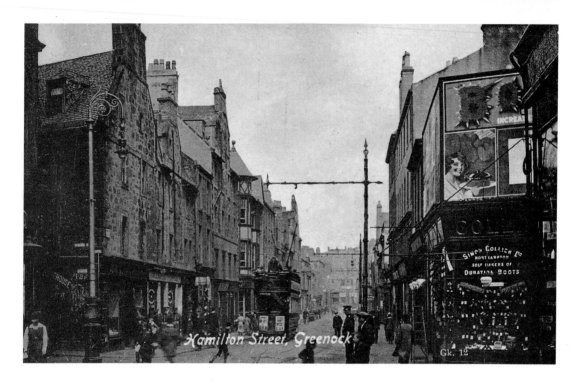

Hamilton Street, Greenock

48. HAMILTON STREET. An open-topped tram is the only traffic visible in this scene from the early 1900s. The premises of Simon Collier Ltd., shoemakers, can be seen on the right of this view. This business was formerly located at 20 Hamilton Street. William Auld in his 'Greenock and its Early Social Environment' relates that the first house in Hamilton Street was built by a tailor and the second by a smith. Evidently these two individuals constantly argued about the name of the street with the tailor, wishing it to be called 'Needle Street', while the smith had a preference for 'Kettle Street'. The magistrates of Greenock at that time took the matter out of the hands of the disputants and named it Hamilton Street, after the Duke of Hamilton. An alternative view is that this street is named after the Hamilton family, who were formerly proprietors of the lands of Finnart. The system of naming streets in Greenock did not come into operation until 1775, when the Town Council passed a resolution which resulted in distinctive names for the streets of the town.

HAMILTON STREET, GREENOCK.

079.

49. HAMILTON STREET. A tram on its way to Port Glasgow proceeds along Hamilton Street in this somewhat misty pre-First World War scene. The shop on the immediate right is the premises of shoemakers Stead and Simpson, who were located at 14 Hamilton Street. The clock shown at this location incorporates the letters which make up the name of the firm and thus provide an ingenious form of advertising. At the same address on the floor above were the premises of Thomas Graham, tailor and clothier. Further along at 20 Hamilton Street, the premises of boot manufacturers Simon Collier Ltd, are partially visible.

Municipal Buildings, Greenock

50. MUNICIPAL BUILDINGS AND CATHCART SQUARE. The site of this square was chosen by Lord Cathcart in the eighteenth century to be the new centre of the town. Fairs were previously held at this location. It was also where twice a year farmers and their wives from the surrounding districts assembled in former times in search of farm-labourers and domestic servants. In 1832 there was a great demonstration in the square following the passing of the Reform Act of that year. Part of the Lyle Fountain can be seen on the bottom right-hand corner of this view. This fountain was presented to the people of Greenock by Provost Abram Lyle in 1879. The fountain was designed by Mr. J.A. Scudamore of Coventry and is decorated with bronze shields of eighteen of the leading families of Greenock. These include Shaw Stewart, Wallace of Kelly, Lyle, Scott, Caird, Fairrie and Crawfurd of Cartsburn.

51. MUNICIPAL BUILDINGS. The size and scale of the Municipal Buildings are seen to advantage in this view. A notable visitor to these civic premises was King George V, who was in Greenock on 17th September 1917. The 'Greenock Telegraph' described the occasion as follows: 'The ceremony in the Town Hall was the outstanding feature of the day's programme and a unique event in the history of Greenock. Reaching the hall by the carriage-drive His Majesty passed into the improvised drawing-room in the area, and was the central figure in a brilliant and memorable scene.' After shaking hands with those who had been presented to him, the King addressed a group of soldiers, who had been wounded in battle, and expressed the hope that they would soon recover. Thereafter, the King proceeded to the Council Chambers, where he remained for a short time before descending the main staircase and re-entering his car in Hamilton Street. Before parting from Provost W.B. McMillan at the Municipal Buildings, His Majesty congratulated him on the excellence of the arrangements made for his visit and asked the Provost to convey to the citizens of Greenock his appreciation of the reception which he had been given. The King also commented on the clean and healthy appearance of the children, who had lined the streets while he had driven through the town.

Court House, Greenock

52. COURT HOUSE. The Sheriff Court in Nelson Street was formally opened shortly before noon on 5th November 1869. Provost Morton was chairman of the proceedings. A large number of the members of the Faculty of Procurators of Greenock and Port Glasgow were also present at this occasion. In addition, there were also representatives from every branch of trade and commerce in Greenock. Provost Morton formally handed over the Sheriff Court to Patrick Fraser, Sheriff of the County, and Hugh L. Tennent, Sheriff Substitute. The Provost stated that the new building was well-planned, commodious and convenient in all its arrangements. He also commended the architects, Messrs. Peddie and Kinnear. Little time was wasted in the Sheriff Court being made fully operational, as at the conclusion of the opening proceedings it was announced by Sheriff Fraser that the first ordinary court would be held within the premises in half an hour. The new Sheriff Court replaced the old Court House, which was built in 1834.

GROSVENOR BOWLING GREEN, GREENOCK

53. GROSVENOR BOWLING GREEN. The Grosvenor Bowling Club was founded on 5th October 1855 at a meeting which was held in Borland's Temperance Hotel, those present being Messrs. William Robinson, Dugald McCall, William Anderson, Peter Campbell, Kenneth Cameron, John Love, James Innes Long, William Gaff and Andrew Dunn. The first Annual General Meeting of the Grosvenor Bowling Club was held on 14th May 1856, when it was reported that the bowling green had been laid out on a site which had been leased from Sir Michael Robert Shaw Stewart. The turf for the green was obtained from Lord Eglinton's Ayrshire estate, as no suitable turf could be found locally. The first office-bearers of the club were as follows: William Robinson, President, 1855-1856; John Erskine, Secretary, 1855-1857; Peter Campbell, Treasurer, 1855-1861. The Grosvenor Bowling Green was officially opened on 17th July 1856. Throughout the first hundred years of its existence the club had a number of significant achievements, which included the winning of the Renfrewshire County Cup in 1882, 1898, 1899, 1900, 1902, 1936 and 1950. The club was named 'Grosvenor' by the founders, as this was the family name of Lady Octavia Shaw Stewart, wife of Sir Michael.

The Bowling Green & Mansion House, Ardgowan Square,

Greenock.

54. ARDGOWAN BOWLING GREEN AND MANSION HOUSE. The flagpole of the Ardgowan Bowling Green has a dominant position in this view. The Mansion House can be seen behind it. This building is located on the north side of Ardgowan Square and at the corner of Partick Street. It was designed by Sir Robert Rowand Anderson (1834-1921) in 1886 and replaced the old Mansion House of the Shaw Stewart family at Well Park after its demolition. The original function of the Mansion House was to serve as estate offices for the Shaw Stewarts. It is built in Dutch Renaissance style and has some interesting architectural features with its elaborate asymetrical doorway, rounded gable and turret. The coat-of-arms of the Shaw Stewarts is carved in stone above the entrance door. The Mansion House provides a continuing link with the Shaw Stewarts and the Old Mansion House which was built more than three hundred years previously. It was described in the Royal Charter of 1635 as 'the auld castell-heid, castle, tour, fortalice and manor place, etc, new buildit'. This description indicates that there was a previous edifice on the site.

Ardgowan Bowling Green, Greenock.

55. ARDGOWAN BOWLING GREEN. In 1841 the Ardgowan Square grounds were granted to a committee of Greenock residents for the promotion of bowling, quoiting and curling, the land originally forming part of the Ardgowan estate. A bowling green of 140 ft square was laid out and also a curling pond 145 ft by 40 ft. In addition, 140 ft of ground was made available for quoiting. Paths were made throughout the grounds, whereby it became possible to walk for almost a mile amongst the shrubbery and flower-beds. A fountain was also built near the centre of the grounds. The curling pond was infilled in 1863 and quoiting was also discontinued. The square is now occupied by bowling greens, tennis courts and gardens.

Greenock.
Holmscroft Schools.

56. HOLMSCROFT SCHOOL. The foundation stone of this school was laid on 26th February 1887 by Mr. (later Sir) Thomas Sutherland, M.P. for Greenock, in the presence of the members of the school board and other local dignitaries including Provost Robert Shankland. Mr. Sutherland tapped the stone with an ebony mallet which had been presented to him and declared the stone to be well and truly laid. He had also been presented with a silver trowel to enable him to spread the mortar. At the ceremony a leaden box containing educational documents, a copy of the programme of the proceedings, and newspapers including the 'Greenock Telegraph' and 'Greenock Herald' were placed under the foundation stone. The proceedings concluded after a choir, conducted by Mr. James Henderson, music master, sang a dedication hymn. This work had been composed and written by Mr. Henderson. Immediately after the ceremony there was a cake and wine banquet in the hall of the adjacent South Parish Church. This distinctive three-storeyed school was demolished in 1968. It was situated at the corner of Ann and Dempster Streets, extending to Wellington Street. The school was originally built to accomodate 1,016 pupils, 236 of whom would be infants.

MEARNS STREET SCHOOL, GREENOCK—ACTION SONG, SENIOR CHOIR, No. 1.
Conductor—Mr. Wm. Carnie.
WINNER OF GOLD MEDAL AND "MERIT" CERTIFICATES—RENFREWSHIRE AND GLASGOW MUSICAL (COMPETITION) FESTIVALS, RESPECTIVELY, 1922.

57. MEARNS STREET SCHOOL. This choir from Mearns Street School achieved high awards in 1922, as indicated on the caption beneath this picture. Mearns Street School was one of four new schools which were built by Greenock School Board, whose members were first elected on 14th April 1873. Such boards were established as a result of the Education (Scotland) Act of 1872. The members of the first Greenock School Board were as follows: Edward Blackmore of Messrs. Rankin and Blackmore, engineers; Dugald Campbell, house factor and accountant; Rev. Dean William Gordon; John Mitchell Hutcheson, sugar broker, Rev. William Laughton, St. Thomas' Free Church; Dr. William Johnstone Marshall; ex-Provost James Morton, iron merchant; Rev. Dr. James Melville McCulloch, West Parish Church; Alexander Mackenzie, editor of the 'Greenock Advertiser'; James Stewart, shipowner; and Dr. James Wallace. Mearns Street School was built to accommodate 795 pupils and the cost of its construction amounted to £11,365 8s.2d. William Cook was the first headmaster of the school and was later appointed to a similar position in Holmscroft School. In addition to holding these positions of responsibility, William Cook also held office as President of the Renfrewshire Branch of the Educational Institute of Scotland.

58. GREENOCK ACADEMY. This imposing building, now demolished, was formerly located in Nelson Street. It was built in 1855 at a cost of £ 7,243. Prior to the building of the school a Corporation Committee had recommended that such an institution should be built by public subscription. In November 1850 a report was submitted from this committee, which stated that the capital of the Academy was to consist of £ 4,000 in 400 shares of £ 10 each. The cost of building the school was assisted by a number of gentlemen who purchased 300 shares. In addition, Mr. William Macfie of Langhouse subscribed £ 1,000, while £ 100 was subscribed by Sir Michael Shaw Stewart, Messrs. Thomas Fairrie, Matthew Brown, Robert Macfie of Airds, John Fairrie and Duncan Hoyle. Mr. John Macfie from Edinburgh gave a donation of £ 100 and £ 50 was received from Mr. Walter Baine. Greenock Academy was opened on 3rd September 1855. It incorporated the grammar school, which had been founded in 1729 and the mathematical school, both of these institutions having been administered by the Town Council. The first rector of Greenock Academy was Robert Buchanan, LL.D. The school became the responsibility of the Greenock School Board in 1882. The present Greenock Academy was built in 1964 and is located in Madeira Street.

The West Kirk, Greenock.

59. THE WEST KIRK. The spire of the West Kirk dominates this view of Nelson Street. Greenock Academy was formely located behind the railings on the left. This site is now occupied by James Watt College with its eight storeys, which was built in 1973. The tower of the Sheriff Court and the spire of St. George's North Church can be seen in this view. The boys on the extreme left and right are barefooted, while the two other boys have footwear and are more smartly dressed. There is also a well-dressed woman who is pushing a pram, beside which there is a child wearing an extremely large hat. The emblem of Greenock with its nautical emphasis and the motto 'God Speed Greenock' can be seen on this postcard.

Old West Kirk, Greenock.

60. OLD WEST KIRK. It is thought that the Old West Kirk was the first Protestant church to have been built in Scotland after the Reformation. On 18th November 1589 at Holyrood House King James VI granted Sir John Shaw of Greenock authority to erect a church for Greenock and its neighbourhood. The church was built and opened for public worship on 5th October 1591. As a result of an Act of Parliament passed on 8th June 1594 this parish was disjoined by Parliament from Inverkip and was designated as the Parish of Greenock, a name which it continued to bear until the erection of the East Parish in 1809. Many of the church's foundation stones were rough boulders, taken from adjacent sea-shore. The church was closed in 1841 because of its uncomfortable and unhealthy condition, having been until that time the Parish Church of Greenock for 250 years and for 150 of these years the only church in Greenock. However, the church was re-opened, after restoration work had been completed at a cost of £ 2,400, on Christmas Day 1864. In 1871 the Old West Kirk was constituted as the North Parish Church. The historic site of this church near the Albert Harbour was acquired by Harland and Wolff shortly after the First World War. In 1926 the Old West Kirk was transferred to its present site on the Esplanade.

Havelock Buildings, Greenock.

61. HAVELOCK BUILDINGS. This view from the early years of the century captures the scene at the corner of West Blackhall Street and Argyle Street. The well-stocked window display in the premises of J.W. Black is particularly eye-catching. These premises were also used as a forwarding office for parcels which were to be carried on the former Caledonian Railway. An estate agency is now located in the premises of this former bookselling and stationery business. The tobacconist's shop on the left is no longer in business and the advertising sign with the figure above it has been removed. An optician is presently located within these premises. An interesting aspect of this scene is that there are figures from all age-groups and, as a result, a variety of fashions of the period are shown to advantage.

CHILDREN'S POND, INVERKIP ROAD, GREENOCK

62. CHILDREN'S POND. A group of children gather at the pond in Lady Alice Park in this scene before the First World War. There are now houses on the higher ground on the opposite side of Inverkip Road. During the formation of the park, advantage was taken to widen and improve the level of Inverkip Road. The work on the six-acre park began on 5th October 1908 and continued until 31st July 1909. After a short interval work was resumed and continued until April 1910. During the first period of the ground being laid out as many as 128 men were employed at one time, and during the second period a total of fifty. The wages paid to these workers amounted to a total of more than £ 4,000, while the cost of material and wages was £ 6,200. At the opening ceremony Lady Alice Shaw Stewart received a solid gold key, which was enamelled with the Shaw Stewart coat-of-arms. This was presented to her by Dean of Guild McCallum on behalf of the Corporation. Mr. McCallum as Convener of the Parks Committee had spent a considerable amount of time in planning the lay-out of the park.

206757 J.V.

Lady Alice Park, Greenock

63. LADY ALICE PARK. This is the Lady Alice Park which is situated to the east of Inverkip Road. Sir Hugh Shaw Stewart presented the fields in 1908 to provide relief work for the increasing number of unemployed. The original intention was that the fields should be set aside wholly for the recreation of children. However, the plan was subsequently modified and two bowling greens were laid out. Additional ground was also made available. This park was named in honour of Lady Alice, wife of Sir Hugh Shaw Stewart.

Union Street, Greenock.

67928 JV

64. UNION STREET. This is a view of a deserted Union Street looking towards George Square. There is not a car nor a horse-drawn vehicle to be seen in this view from the early years of this century. This is certainly a contrast to the present time with the large volume of traffic which is to be seen in Union Street. The high quality of the terraced houses and the well-laid pavements with the trees spaced at regular intervals, demonstrates the planned nature of this part of the West End of the town. Many of the mansions in Union Street were built by the merchants and shipbuilders of Greenock in the early 1800s. The lamp-posts shown here have been removed. On the right of the picture the figure of a maid is just visible, this being at a time when domestic servants would be employed in considerable numbers by families who resided in this part of the town.

Union Street.   Greenock.

wishing you the Compliments of the Season JHHyndman

2698. 6.

65. UNION STREET. This postcard has been used to send Christmas greetings, having been posted on 23rd December 1905. In this view it can be seen that part of Union Street has a cobblestone surface. Three prominent buildings are visible, these being St. John's Episcopal Church on the left, St. George's North Church in the centre and the twin towers of the Watt Library, one of which is partially obscured by trees. The 19th century mansions on the left of the picture still remain, but are not used for residential purposes. The absence of traffic in this early 20th century is in marked contrast to the present time. In this view a lone cyclist and a horse and cart are the only traffic to be seen.

Greenock *George Square*

66. GEORGE SQUARE. The tower of St. George's North Church dominates this view of a deserted George Square in the early 1900s. This church was built by Salmon Son and Ritchie in 1870-1871. It was originally the Free Middle Church, becoming successively a United Free congregation and finally a Church of Scotland congregation. This church, which was designed to seat 1,050 persons, was formally opened for public worship on 11th June 1871, when a large congregation were present at a service conducted by the Rev. Dr. William Buchanan. Afternoon and evening services were also held on that day. It was announced at the evening service that the day's total collection amounted to just over £1,000. A contemporary newspaper report stated the following regarding this matter: 'The largeness of the sum evidently astonished the congregation, through which a subdued murmur was heard to run.' At the time of its construction this church tower at a height of 200 feet, 9 inches was the tallest structure in Greenock by 13 feet.

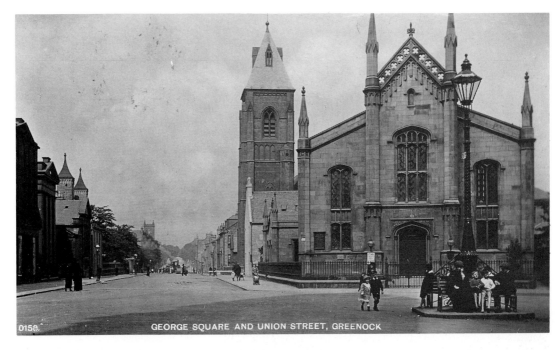

GEORGE SQUARE AND UNION STREET, GREENOCK

67. GEORGE SQUARE AND UNION STREET. George Square was formerly known as Kilblain Square, but when improvements were made here in 1789 it was decided that it would be named after the reigning monarch, who at that time was King George III. Union Street is so named because it relates to the Act of Union between the United Kingdom of Great Britain and Ireland, which took place in 1801. This street was previously known as the High Road, which led to Gourock through open countryside with crops growing in the fields. The twin towers of the Watt Library are visible on the left of this picture. In the centre the tower of St. John's Episcopal Church can be seen. George Square Congregational Church is on the right of this view. There is a plaque on the exterior wall to the left of the church door, which indicates that it marks the resting-place of the Rev. Alexander Campbell, who was the minister here when the church was opened in 1840. Mr. Campbell died only four years after this event at the early age of 34. This church was designed by John Baird I in the architectural style known as Pinnacled Perpendicular. The tall lamp-post and seating on the right have been removed and this area is now used for car parking.

NELSON STREET, GREENOCK.

68. NELSON STREET. A barefooted boy stands in front of the lamp-post in a traffic-free Nelson Street. The lamp-post has been removed and this location is now a busy roundabout. On the left of this view a group of women and children can be seen. This group includes a small boy with a large bicycle! The premises of Nelson Street Post Office are located between the little girl on the left and the baby in the pram. There is an air of peace and tranquillity in this street-scene of long ago when compared to the present time with a constant traffic flow. However, all of the buildings shown here remain in position and the tenements on the right have recently been modernised.

NELSON STREET, GREENOCK.

69. NELSON STREET. This is a view of the tenements in Nelson Street looking from Inverkip Road. The road to the right is Inverkip Street. Part of Orangefield Baptist Church can be seen on the right of this view. This church was built in 1879 and was designed by Thomas McLelland. This tranquil scene is in marked contrast to the present day. There is now a roundabout at the very location where the horse and wagon are in this view. This street was named in honour of Horatio, Lord Nelson (1758-1805). Daniel Weir in his 'History of the Town of Greenock' mentions that Lord Nelson was carried to the cockpit of the 'Victory' by a Greenock seaman after being fatally wounded at the Battle of Trafalgar in 1805. A few months after the battle this seaman appeared before the audience of the theatre which then stood in Mansionhouse Lane. He related the events surrounding the Battle of Trafalgar and the details of Nelson's death. Lord Nelson is also commemorated by Nile Street, which is named after the Battle of the Nile, when he succeeded in ending Napoleon's ambitions in the Near East in 1798. The naval battle in which he was killed is commemorated by Trafalgar Street.

The West Kirk, Greenock. RELIABLE SERIES.

70. THE WEST KIRK. This church in Nelson Street was built between 1839 and 1841, the architect being David Cousin. The elegant spire was added in 1854. It occupies a commanding position and is seen to advantage from Brisbane Street. The belfry of this church contains the original bell of 1677, which was formerly in the Old West Kirk. The new West Kirk was built because the Old West Kirk had fallen into disrepair. In 1912 a refurbisment of the interior of the church was undertaken with a chancel being added by John Keppie. On 27th April 1966 this church united with Greenock Gaelic Church and became known as the Old Kirk. The Rev. Patrick MacFarlan (1781-1849), who became minister of the West Kirk in 1832, was elected Moderator of the General Assembly of the Church of Scotland in 1834. He joined the Free Church of Scotland at the Disruption inn 1843 and was minister of the West Free Church, Greenock from 1843 to 1849. Patrick MacFarlan became Moderator of the Free Church of Scotland in 1845. Another notable minister of this church was the Rev. James Melville McCulloch (1802-1883). He became minister in 1843 and had been a headmaster at an early age before entering the Church. His 'Course of Reading' was the most notable school-book of its time. This church is now known as St. Luke's Church.

GARDENS, AUCHMOUNTAIN GLEN, GREENOCK

71. GARDENS, AUCHMOUNTAIN GLEN. A figure of Lord Nelson can be seen at the top of the steps of these gardens. Until the mid-1880s Auchmountain Glen was a beauty spot of which Greenockians were justifiably proud, its main attraction being a spring of cooling water. It was during the great trade depression in 1887, when Sir Michael Shaw Stewart gave permission for local men to make a pathway through the Glen from Kilmacolm Road to Whinhill. Men from the east end of the town were particularly enthusiastic about this project and they received materials from many shipyards and local firms. These men, known as the 'Glen Boys', began to collect figureheads from ships, busts, cast-iron guns and flagpoles to put on display in the Glen. The 'Glen Boys' also built a greenhouse and grew plants, the result of which transformed the Glen into a blaze of colour, making it a place of beauty which was unique among Scottish towns. Formerly, each 'boy' received a small subsidy from the Corporation of Greenock and was required to work two full nights each week in the Glen. However, housing schemes have been built on both sides of the Glen and thus its rural character was lost.

72. CLUB HOUSE, AUCHMOUNTAIN GLEN. This view shows the Club House and committee rooms which formerly stood in Auchmountain Glen. The evidence of the work of the 'Glen Boys' is visible in this picture. These men from the east end of the town cleaned the bed of the stream in the glen, built sluices, a dam and waterfalls. In its heyday in the 1930s bus parties picknicked in the glen, but later on the number of visitors declined with the encroachment of nearby housing schemes. In the early 1960s the author of the town's entry in the Third Statistical Account wrote the following regarding the condition of Auchmountain Glen: 'The paths are weedy, the statuary is mossy, the burn is choked and cluttered with rubbish, the railings are rickety and the bridges perilous.' He expressed the hope that the glen would be restored to its former glory. More than thirty years later, in April 1994, the glen was reopened after the first phase of a restoration project. This was made possible by grant assistance of £150,000 from the Scottish Conservation Project's Trust, the European Social Fund, Inverclyde District Council, Renfrewshire Enterprise, Strathclyde Regional Council and Scottish Natural Heritage.

73. AUCHMOUNTAIN GLEN. A well-dressed gent looks on as his companion is about to take some water from one of the wells in the glen in the early 1900s. This was one of the two wells in the vicinity at which the busts of Sir Walter Scott, Robert Burns and James Watt were placed in 1887. The other well in the glen had a built-in subscription box. This view shows the former condition of the glen with a well-laid footpath in evidence. There was formerly an Auchmountain Boys' Society, the object of which was to maintain Auchmountain Glen as a public facility by keeping roads, bridges and seats in good order. Finance for the maintenance of the glen was raised by public subscription and by raising funds from concerts and cruises.

Wellpark & Victoria Tower, Greenock.

74. WELL PARK AND VICTORIA TOWER. Well Park was presented to the town in 1851 by Sir Michael Shaw Stewart. This view from the early 1900s shows the park before the War Memorial was built. The site of the park was formerly the garden of the old Greenock Mansion House, which was vacated and demolished in 1886, having been acquired by the Caledonian Railway Company, in order to undertake tunnelling work for the extension of their line to Gourock. The old Mansion House was built by the eighth John Schaw in 1542. Until the time of its demolition it was still possible to decipher dates on stones connected with the building as within its interior the dates 1635 and 1674 could be seen at different locations. For generations this edifice was the residence of the Schaw and latterly the Shaw Stewart families. Prior to the industrial development of Greenock the policies of the Mansion House were large and extensive, stretching eastward and westward in luxuriant plantations, running southward to Whinhill and northward to the shores of the Clyde. The latest addition to the old Mansion House took place in 1740 when the builder was James Watt, father of Greenock's most famous son. Much regret was expressed in the town when this historic building was demolished.

In Well Park, Greenock.

75. WELL PARK. The small structure on the right bears the date 1629 and is still in position in Well Park. Is was from this well that spring water was supplied to the old Greenock Mansion House. The initials of John Schaw and his wife with their coats-of-arms are also inscribed on this historic structure. The Victoria Tower dominates this scene in Well Park, which has been a place of recreation for the people of Greenock since the middle of the nineteenth century.

The Well Park, Greenock

76. THE WELL PARK. The spire of Wellpark Church dominates this view of the park. This church was designed by J.J.M. and W.H. Hay in 1853-1854. Sadly as a result of vandalism the building is now in a ruinous condition. The congregation, who were formerly Original Secession, joined the Church of Scotland in 1839, but left to join the Free Church of Scotland at the Disruption in 1843. The first minister of this Free Church congregation was the Rev. James Stark, who served from 1843 until 1890. The Rev. Matthew Reid was appointed as a minister in 1873 and served until 1903. He was also clerk to the Presbytery of Greenock from 1900 until 1919.

H.M. Royal Naval Torpedo Factory, Greenock   360

77. **H.M. ROYAL NAVAL TORPEDO FACTORY.** The main structure of the factory was a one-storey building, which covered about 6,000 yards. There were special arrangements made for transporting the torpedoes to a jetty for shipment. Torpedoes were stored in the War Office property at Fort Matilda, to which there was a subway from the factory. At the end of the First World War all the torpedo factories in the country were closed. However, in 1921, the Government gave £ 10,000 to re-build this factory. Torpedoes were also manufactured here during the Second World War. The factory was later known as H.M. Torpedo Experimental Establishment and was finally closed in 1959.

Men leaving the Torpedo Factory, Greenock

78. MEN LEAVING THE TORPEDO FACTORY. This factory was formerly located at the Battery Park. In 1907 the Admiralty compulsorily acquired several acres of land from Sir Hugh Shaw Stewart for £ 27,225. In a letter to the Corporation of Greenock at that time Sir Hugh enclosed a cheque for £ 5,000 of the purchase price, which was to be spent to benefit the town of Greenock. He believed that the financial gain should be of benefit to the community, as Battery Park had been common land for local people for generations and should be preserved. Batttery Park was handed over to the Corporation of Greenock in 1914. The site of the Clyde Torpedo Factory amounted to 10 acres of land and 4.75 acres of foreshore. The original buildings of the factory were opened in 1910, the cost being in the region of £ 30,000.

79. JAMES REID. James Reid (1839-1908) was Conservative M.P. for Greenock from 1900 until 1906. He was educated at Belfast Academy and Queen's University, Belfast. At a later period he was Chairman of Fleming, Reid and Company Ltd., worsted spinners and hosiery manufacturers, which was based in Greenock. In 1900 James Reid was appointed as Honorary Colonel in the 1st Renfrew and Dumbarton Royal Garrison Artillery (Volunteers). He was also a Past Provincial Grand Master of Freemasonry of Renfrewshire West. In addition, he held office as a Justice of the Peace and was a former Deputy Lieutenant for the County of Renfrew. James Reid married Jessie Ryburn Galbreath, daughter of Greenock merchant John Galbreath, in 1872. However, his wife pre-deceased him in 1899. James Reid resided at Monfode, Greenock.

JAS. REID, ESQ., J.P., D.L.
M.P. for Greenock.

Greta Series.

80. MERINO MILLS. The Merino Mills in Drumfrochar Road were formerly the premises of Fleming, Reid and Co., the founders being John Fleming and James Reid, who built a small spinning mill in 1840 and took five falls on the aqueduct of the Cart from the Shaws Water Company. However, it was not until 1890 that the firm began to spin knitting wool from Australian merinos. The first large mill was destroyed by fire in 1880, but was rebuilt on the same site, a task which took two years. During that period the business of the company was temporarily carried on in England. This view shows these new buildings, which were 220 ft in length, 60 ft in breadth and occupied six storeys. In addition, there were knitting sheds, warehouses and washhouses. This company had an excellent reputation as spinners of carpet yarns, but it also became well-known for tweed yarns, as dress piece makers for Bradford and braid makers for Manchester. Fleming, Reid and Co. formerly supplied their products direct to the public via the 380 branches of the Scottish Wool and Hosiery Stores, which were located throughout the U.K. Three of these stores were in Greenock, these being located in West Blackhall Street, Rue End Street and Drumfrochar Road. Even by 1959 nearly 1,000 women and 150 men were employed by this company, but operations have now ceased.

GREENOCK FIRE BRIGADE.

JONES PHOTO.

81. GREENOCK FIRE BRIGADE. A group of men from the Greenock Fire Brigade are seen with their first motorised fire-engine which began service in the town in 1912. On 15th November of that year Greenock Corporation acquired the four-ton vehicle, which had been purchased for £ 1,085 from Dennis Bros. of Guildford, Surrey. On the same day there was a demonstration of the workings of the fire-engine at the west end of the Esplanade. The powerful turbine-pump worked extremely well on this occasion and the jets of water reached 80 feet in height. This demonstration was observed by a number of people, which included members of Greenock Corporation and employers. At the conclusion of the hour-long event the invited guests went by reserved tramcar to Cathcart Square, where they adjourned for lunch to the Harbour Trust Room at which Councillor Orr presided. He was then Convener of the Committee of Management of the Fire Brigade. In 1912 the Fire Brigade was based at the Municipal Buildings in Dalrymple Street and operated on a 24-hour basis. The Brigade Superintendent at that time was William Taylor.

BEDFORD STREET, GREENOCK.

82. BEDFORD STREET. The substantial detached villa on the right of this view is known as 'The Limes'. It is located at No. 1 Newark Street. This view dates from the early years of the present century and has not greatly altered. The West End of the town was originally planned by David Reid, who was employed on this task in 1818. Many large mansions were built, which gave this part of the town an air of prosperity. However, Reid's plans took over a century to complete, but much of it remains as he planned it. The formation of a purely residential area was due to the desire of people to move away from the unhealthy atmosphere in poorly-ventilated houses in the centre of Greenock, an accumulation of wealth by certain families and an availability of suitable sites on which to build new properties.

Toll House, Greenock

Copyright. Gk.47.

83. TOLL HOUSE. In past centuries Eldon Street was close to the shore, and it was the only road to Gourock. If high tides occurred, it was not possible to reach Gourock until the weather changed. Turnpike roads were established in Scotland in 1750 and there was originally a toll-bar in Eldon Street, at Cardwell Bay. It was there that tolls were collected from all carriages, carts and other horse-drawn vehicles which used the road. These tolls were used to finance road maintenance. However, the income from the toll-bars was not always sufficient to provide adequate road maintenance. For example, this occurred between Whitsunday 1810 and 1811, when the income from all the toll-bars in Renfrewshire, amounting to £ 10,300, was inadequate for such purposes. Mail coaches which used the turnpike roads regularly were exempted from paying any toll, and thus the income was reduced. Toll-bars in Renfrewshire were not abolished until 1882. In this view the Toll House in Eldon Street can be seen. It is now known as the Old Toll House.

INVERKIP ROAD, GREENOCK.

84. INVERKIP ROAD. A solitary vehicle is just visible on Inverkip Road in this scene from over sixty years ago. Nowadays it is an extremely busy road. Part of the Lady Alice Park can be seen on the left of this view. In 1803 Sir John Shaw Stewart made the first turnpike road from Inverkip through the Kip Valley to Greenock. In order to build this road, the course of the River Kip had to be altered and much masonry was used. In past centuries the Parish of Inverkip included Greenock and Port Glasgow. In 1589 a petition was presented by 'the fishers of Greenock' to have a church of their own. They complained of the long journey they had to make to and from the old church of Inverkip, leaving no time for rest on Sundays 'according to Goddis institution'. In 1591 their wish for a church was granted when the Old West Kirk was built.

Tontine Hotel, Greenock.

85. TONTINE HOTEL. The Tontine Hotel was originally built as a private residence in 1808 for George Robertson, who was a Senior Magistrate in the town and a leading partner of the Newfoundland trading firm of Hunter, Robertson and Company. It is thought that George Robertson was the first person in Greenock to own a private carriage and to possess a piano. He also played a large part in the Shaws Water Scheme, which was completed in 1827. The main purpose of this scheme was to encourage industrial expansion and supply power to the mills. In 1892 the proprietor of the original Tontine Hotel in Cathcart Street moved to Ardgowan Square, where he continued in business in George Robertson's former residence. A porch was later added and thus the original entry is now hidden from view. The site of this hotel was previously occupied by a windmill for grinding corn. George Robertson's mansion was shown as the most westerly building in Greenock in a water-colour which was painted soon after its erection.

ON THE CUT, GREENOCK

0156

86. THE CUT. In 1811 a new reservoir known as Town's Dam was built, but it was soon found to be insufficient for the increased demands from Greenock's industries and population. Robert Thom made a major contribution in improving the town's water supply. He was a civil engineer and proprietor of the Rothesay Cotton Works. It was in 1824 when Sir Michael Shaw Stewart asked Robert Thom to survey the ground above Greenock. Robert Thom was the engineer of the Shaws Water Joint Stock Company, which was incorporated by an Act of Parliament on 10th June 1825. His plan was to form an immense artificial loch 2 miles from Greenock and lead the water along the hills at an elevation of more than 500 feet above sea-level, until the point when it approached the town it should be made to cascade down successive falls in order that water-power could be used in local industries. The result was the reservoir known as Loch Thom with a capacity of 1,780 million gallons and the aqueduct known as the 'Cut' which amounted to 5 ½ miles in length. This scenic walk has been enjoyed by successive generations of Greenock people and many others.

206766 J.V.

The Cut, Greenock

87. THE CUT. The Cut was officially opened on 16th April 1827. On that day at a quarter to twelve the sluices were raised by the Chief Magistrate, William Leitch, who entered a boat and was floated along on the first tide of the stream in its new and artificial channel. It later arrived at Everton near Greenock at 2.45 p.m., where it was received with cheers and a salute of cannon. The water was then allowed to flow into the regulating basin for forty-five minutes. It was at this point that the stream took its descending course. At 3.30 p.m. the sluice was opened by Sir Michael Shaw Stewart and the water then cascaded down each successive fall. The 'Greenock Advertiser' reported as follows: 'It was at this juncture that the scene became one of the most interesting and animated description. The spectators who amounted to several thousands, but who had previously been scattered irregularly over a considerable extent of the aqueduct line, now became more condensed and moved onwards as if in procession, following the march of the stream.' After having supplied water to Greenock for 141 years, the Cut was replaced in 1971 by a 1 ¼ mile tunnel from Loch Thom to Long Dam at Overton.

UPPER GREENOCK STATION.

88. UPPER GREENOCK STATION. This postcard of the station was sent on 8th August 1914, which was only four days after Britain had declared war on Germany. Originally this was a station of the Greenock and Wemyss Bay Railway Company, which opened on 13th May 1865. Three years earlier, in 1862, a group of Greenock businessmen secured an Act to build a railway line between Port Glasgow and Wemyss Bay. The route of the new ten-mile railway began a short distance west of Port Glasgow station, rose up the hill face behind Greenock via Inverkip to Wemyss Bay. However, the new railway was not immediately successful, due to the inexperience of staff in the working of a single line. There were also the problems of a tunnel collapse and a rock-fall. A further handicap was that passengers did not travel on the line and continued to travel on the Greenock trains, with the result that the new Wemyss Bay steamers were withdrawn. Matters improved greatly in 1869, when Captain Alexander Campbell resigned from the Anchor Line to assume the management of the Wemyss Bay Steamboat Company. On 1st August 1893 the Greenock and Wemyss Bay Railway Company, which had remained nominally independent, amalgamated with the Caledonian Railway Company.

89. BOAT CLUBHOUSE. An old Greenock 'worthy' stands near the Royal West of Scotland Amateur Boat Clubhouse at the west end of the Esplanade in the early 1900s. Another figure is just visible looking out of the window in the centre of the building. One of the most important nautical events in the calendar in former years was the Clyde Fortnight, which was organised by the Clyde yacht clubs and took place in the first half of July. It is recorded that on 11th July 1891 seventy yachts participated in the Royal Clyde Yacht Club's Regatta. There was considerable public interest shown in the large yachts in the 1890s and it was usual for crowds to gather at strategic points on shore to watch them racing. It also became the custom for one or more of the Clyde steamers to be chartered as 'Club Steamer' during the Clyde Fortnight. The Caledonian Steam Packet Company's 'Duchess of Hamilton' was used more often than any other vessel in these duties. On a further nautical theme Greenock has a good record in the sport of rowing. The Cartsdyke Worthies' are considered to be the most famous of all the Greenock oarsmen. They were T. Smillie, J. Calderhead, W. Calderhead and J. Moodie.

Greenock. From Golf Course.

M. 195

90. GREENOCK FROM THE GOLF COURSE. This is a view of the clubhouse of Greenock Golf Club which dates from the beginning of this century, when a course was laid out at the Battery. The fiftieth anniversary of the founding of this club was marked by the presentation of a silver cigar box, which was to be competed for annually by members over sixty-five years of age. There is also the Whinhill Golf Course, which was laid out by William Fernie of Troon. The official opening ceremony of this course took place on 7th April 1911, when in addition to the invited guests there was a crowd of a thousand people who were present in the vicinity of the clubhouse. The official guests were Dean of Guild McCallum, Sir Hugh and Lady Alice Shaw Stewart, Provost and Mrs. McMillan, ex-Bailie Williamson, Councillor W.H. Carmichael, W.D. Low, William Fernie and Harry Fernie. In his speech the Dean of Guild pointed out that over forty years previously, the then Police Board of Greenock leased the Whinhill from Sir Michael Shaw Stewart as a recreation ground for the inhabitants of the town at a rent of £ 50 a year. When it was the time for the lease to be renewed about two years previously it was the opinion of the Parks Committee that permission be sought from Sir Hugh Shaw Stewart for golf to be played on this site.

91. HIGHLAND MARY MONUMENT. This monument was erected in memory of Highland Mary, her real name being Mary Campbell. She became famous because of ther romantic association with Robert Burns, Scotland's National Bard. On 14th May 1789 Mary Campbell and Robert Burns went through a form of marriage ceremony on the banks of the Fail, a tributary of the Ayr, in which they exchanged bibles, washed their hands in the water and plighted their troth. In October of the same year Mary died of typhoid fever at the early age of 22, while lodging with relations at 31 Upper Charles Street in Greenock. A plaque in High Street opposite Buccleugh Street now marks the site of the house where she died. After her death Mary Campbell was buried in the Old West Kirk Yard. In 1842 the monument in this view was erected over her grave. On 13th November 1920 her remains were re-interred in Greenock Cemetery after an impressive religious ceremony in which members of the Greenock Burns Club carried the bier. The monument was also relocated there. It is of significance that Greenock Burns Club is one of the oldest of its type in the world, having been founded in 1801.

Custom House Quay

Greenock

92. CUSTOM HOUSE QUAY. Part of the Custom House is visible on the right of this view. This building was designed by William Burn in 1818, and is considered to be one of the finest custom houses in Britain. The construction of the Custom House was financed by the Government at a cost of £33,000, with the aim that it would be the centre for Greenock's growing overseas trade. The tall structure on the quay is the Beacon Fountain, which was designed by local marine artist William Clark and incorporates a clock, beacon light and weather vane. There was formerly a waiting-room for ship passengers in the building on the left. Within these premises there was also the Towing Office of the Glasgow and Greenock Shipping Company and the office of the Glasgow, Dublin and Londonderry Steam Packet Company. Custom House Quay was also known as the Old Steamboat Quay. A decision to add a new eastern arm to the East Quay was made in 1788 and this work was carried out at a cost of £3,840, this sum covering the cost of the eastward extension and the reconstruction of the westward arm of the East Quay. When these improvements were completed it was discovered that a rock known as the 'Leo' prevented the access of vessels to the quay and as a result a new contract for work to cover this obstruction was made in 1791.

GREENOCK, CUSTOM HOUSE QUAY

93. CUSTOM HOUSE QUAY. A steamer approaches Custom House Quay in this interesting scene. The Glasgow, Paisley and Green-ock Railway, which was opened in 1841, had a terminus close to Custom House Quay, where many up-river steamers called. The railway company soon came to an agreement with the Bute Steam Packet Company, whereby their vessels 'Isle of Bute' and 'Maid of Bute' would sail in connection with the trains. In 1844 the Glasgow, Paisley and Greenock Railway Company took over direct control of the steamers, an additional three of which were purchased. However, this move resulted in considerable opposition from private steamboat owners operating from Glasgow. Losses were incurred and in 1846 the steamers were sold. In 1851 the Glasgow, Paisley and Greenock Railway was absorbed into the Caledonian Railway. Custom House Quay became the Caledonian Railway's principal outlet to the expanding traffic on the upper Firth and provided connections with various steamer owners. When Prince's Pier was opened in 1869 a gradual decline began of steamers calling at Custom House Quay. It is thought that the last regular Clyde steamer which called here was the 'Mercury' (1892) on her mid-day Kyles run on 30th June 1915. Until 1962 coastal and West Highland vessels called at the quay.

The Lyle Road, Greenock

This is a view of a very pretty place in Greenock. Do write me a nice long letter soon, my dear. It is not Hyle Street, it is Lyle Street I stay in. Your very sincere Cousin Chrissie Gibb.

94. THE LYLE ROAD. The construction of the Lyle Road took place during 1878-1880, when there was high unemployment in the town. The work on this project began on 3rd December 1878 with 31 men working from 8 a.m. till 4 p.m. at the rate of less than 10p per day. By 31st December 1878 the number of men employed was 378, but during the spring of 1879 this figure was reduced to 350 men, while an average of 280 men were employed on the project during the summer and autumn of the same year. By May 1880 the number of those employed had been further reduced to 160 men. A total of forty stone-breakers also worked on the project. The official opening ceremony took place on 1st May 1880. After the ceremony the official party adjourned to a wooden shed in the vicinity of the Craigs farm, where according to a contemporary newspaper report 'a repast of a thoroughly rustic kind had been prepared'. This consisted of curds and cream, fresh butter, cheese, home-baked oatmeal cake and scones. The road is named after Abram Lyle, who was Provost of Greenock when the project was commenced.

Lyle Road. Greenock.

95. THE LYLE ROAD. The cost of building the Lyle Road was about £13,000, £2,000 of which were for plant and material. Instead of earth slopes being used to keep the embankments in position, several very heavy stone walls were built. These took up less ground and provided increased stability. At the top of Lyle Hill heavy walls were also built and additional slopes were formed in order to provide the public with fine views from that location. There were problems with the ground on the west side of the hill and this involved considerable expenditure for drainage work and rebuilding the road after landslides. An additional problem in the building of the Lyle Road was that most of the men who were involved in its construction were inexperienced in this type of work, many of them being old and not physically fit. However, these men were kept constantly at work on the exposed site of Lyle Hill throughout severe winter weather.

THE HOSPITAL, GATESIDE, GREENOCK.

96. THE HOSPITAL GATESIDE. In 1899 it was suggested by the Medical Officer of Health for Greenock, Dr. James Wallace, that there was a need not only for additional hospital accommodation, but for a new hospital to be located on a site away from Greenock Infirmary. Nine years later, in January 1908, the Greenock and District Combination Hospital costing £ 70,000 was opened at Gateside. The ten-acre site for the hospital cost £ 5,500. The first Superintendent of the Combination Hospital was Dr. Andrew Love. This hospital served the population of Greenock, Port Glasgow, Gourock and the western part of Renfrewshire. There were a total of 120 beds in the separate pavilion system for five classes of infectious diseases, these being enteric fever, typhus fever, measles, diptheria and scarlet fever. There was also provision in separate buildings for the isolation of patients with double infection and the special treatment of patients prior to their discharge from hospital. The architect of the hospital was Alexander Cullen, F.R.I.B.A.

Smithston War Hospital, N.B.

71975. JV.

97. SMITHSTON WAR HOSPITAL. This hospital in Inverkip Road was used as a military hospital for soldiers during the First World War. At the beginning of the Second World War in 1939, the hospital was requisitioned by the Admiralty. Two years later in 1941, the Canadian Navy took over the hospital, which was renamed HMCS 'Niobe,' the former patients having been moved to other hospitals. This building was originally known as the Smithston Poorhouse and Asylum and was erected during 1876-1879, the architect being John Starforth. It was built on land which had formerly belonged to the farm of Smithston. Eighty-three acres were purchased at a cost of £ 7,000. The total cost of building the Smithston Poorhouse and Asylum was £ 122,904. The Earl of Mar and Kellie laid the foundation stone of the building in September 1876 and the opening ceremony was performed by Mr. James Stewart, M.P. for the Burgh of Greenock, on 29th March 1879. There was much adverse criticism of the cost of this institution. This found expression in the columns of the 'Greenock Telegraph' and the 'Greenock Advertiser' at that time. In 1948 when the National Health Service came into being this institution was renamed Ravenscraig Hospital.

PRINTED BY M'KELVIE, GREENOCK.   MARINERS' ASYLUM, GREENOCK.   PHOTO BY G. A. BROWN, GREENOCK

98. MARINERS' ASYLUM. The Mariners' Asylum in Newark Street was opened on 17th October 1854. It was founded by Sir Gabriel Wood, who was born in Greenock on 19th May 1767, and died in Bath on 29th October 1845. He joined the civil service and in 1796 was appointed as Vice-Consul for the State of Maryland, U.S.A. He was later appointed as Commissary-General of Accounts in Canada. All his life Sir Gabriel was generous in his contributions to charities in Greenock. In particular, he felt that there was a need for an institution for aged and destitute seamen. In his will he left the whole of his residuary estate to his wife and sister in order that such an institution could be erected and endowed. The Mariners' Asylum was built on a seven-acre site and was designed in the collegiate Tudor style by D. Mackintosh. At the outset if provided accommodation for fifty merchant master mariners and merchant seamen in necessitous circumstances who had to be over 55 years of age and be of good character. A further requirement was that these men had to have been born in the counties of Renfrew, Ayr, Dumbarton, Argyll or Bute. In 1921 the name of this institution was changed to Mariners' Home Incorporated.

THE FRENCH MEMORIAL, LYLE HILL, GREENOCK,
CARDWELL BAY AND GOUROCK IN BACKGROUND.

A. 9709.

99. THE FREE FRENCH MEMORIAL. This memorial with the sculptured Cross of Lorraine occupies a dominant position on Lyle Hill overlooking the Firth of Clyde. A plaque records that it is dedicated to the memory of the Free French Naval Forces who sailed from Greenock in the years 1940-1945 and died in the Battle of the Atlantic for the liberation of France and the success of the Allied cause. It was designed and erected by the officers and men of the French Naval Base at Greenock with the help of subscriptions raised from the crews of the Free French Naval Forces. There are three further plaques on this memorial. These read as follows: 1. 'To the memory of Captain de Frigate Blaison, the officers and crew of the submarine "Surcouf", lost in the Atlantic, February 1947'; 2. 'To the memory of the Captains, officers and crew of the corvettes "Alysee" and "Mimosa" which disappeared in the Battle of the Atlantic, 1942'; 3. 'To the Memory of the Free French Naval Forces who never ceased the struggle and fell gloriously for the liberation of the honour of France and for history.'

100. GREENOCK FROM LYLE ROAD. This is a view of Greenock in the 1900s. In 1901 the population of the town was 68,217, the figure a century earlier having been 17,458. In 1841 Greenock's population amounted to 36,986, much of this increase being due to people moving from the Highlands and Ireland. A further increase occured between 1850 and 1880 as a result of the development of the railways and increased industrialisation. In 1900 very few births took place in hospital. Even by 1928 only 5.5 per cent of total births took place in hospital. Infectious diseases were prevalent at the beginning of the century. In 1900 within the town there were ten deaths from typhoid, eleven from scarlet fever, seventy-four from whooping cough and twenty-two from diptheria.

SHERIFF BUILDINGS, NELSON STREET, GREENOCK.

E 02870

101. NELSON STREET. A motor-cyclist with sidecar proceeds along Nelson Street in this scene. The Sheriff Court is on the right of this view with the imposing spire of St. George's North Church to its left. Straight ahead is George Square Baptist Church, which was built by James Sellars in 1888.

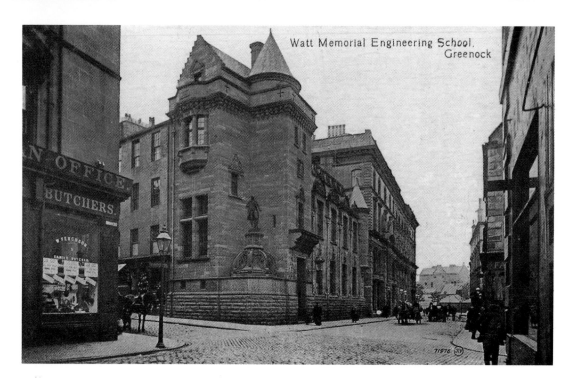

Watt Memorial Engineering School.
Greenock

102. WATT MEMORIAL ENGINEERING SCHOOL. The Watt Memorial Engineering School in William Street and Dalrymple Street was built in 1908. It was designed by H. and D. Barclay in the Scots Renaissance style. Andrew Carnegie, the great Scottish philanthropist, established a fund to erect this building with a contribution of £ 10,000. The school marks the site of the house in which James Watt was born in 1736. However, this house was demolished in the closing years of the eighteenth century. The pedestalled bronze statue of James Watt by H.C. Fehr is visible at the north-east corner of the building. Marine engineering and navigation were formerly taught at this establishment, which finally closed in 1973 when the new James Watt College was opened in Nelson Street. The tenement buiding to the left of the school in William Street is Greenock's oldest surviving residential property having been built in 1752. All of the buildings on the extreme right of this view have been demolished and this is where Rue End Street is now situated.

Greenock from the Harbour.

103. GREENOCK FROM THE HARBOUR. The Victoria Tower dominates this view of the West Harbour. The building of this harbour commenced in 1907, when gardeners and masons were brought from Edinburgh, the former being employed in Scotland at that time for excavating work. The West Harbour and quays were completed in 1710 at a cost of £ 5,555 11s 1d. The harbour was described in 1711 as being 'a most commodious, safe and good harbour, having 18 feet depth at spring tide'. In 1710 the historian Crawfurd wrote that Greenock was the 'chief town upon the coast, well built, consisting chiefly of one principal street, about a quarter of a mile in length'. The population of the parish of Greenock is estimated to have been about 2,000 at the beginning of the eighteenth century. This figure had increased to 4,100 by 1735, with 2,983 of this number residing in the town of Greenock.

104. WEST HARBOUR AND MID QUAY. A variety of craft rest at anchor in this picturesque scene of the West Harbour and Mid Quay in former years. The West Harbour came into use in 1710, the same year in which Greenock was established as a custom-house port. As a result of this there was a rapid increase in foreign trade. This situation irritated the merchants of London, Liverpool, Bristol and Whitehaven, as they found that their trade links with Europe were being cut. These merchants attempted to prove that Greenock was favoured by collusion between the customs officials and merchants of the town. A bill was introduced in Parliament to remove the foreign trade privileges of Greenock and it required the raising of the matter in the House of Commons by Scottish M.P.s to maintain Greenock's custom house. However, the customs officers at Greenock were removed from their positions and replaced by a new group of men.

105. WATT LIBRARY. This library is located in Union Street. Although the building was incomplete, the library opened in 1837. James Watt's son, also named James Watt, donated £ 3,500 towards building costs. A white marble statue of James Watt, designed by Sir Francis Chantrey, was installed in 1838. The inscription on the base of the statue written by Lord Jeffrey reads as follows: 'The inhabitants of Greenock have erected this statue of James Watt, not to extend a fame already identified with the miracles of steam, but to testify the pride and reverence with which he is remembered in the place of his nativity and their deep sense of the great benefits his genius had conferred on mankind.' At that time £ 3,457 had been spent on the construction of the centre buildings according to the original plan by Edward Blore. The building of the Watt Library was completed by 1846. The reasons for its foundation were as follows: to preserve the books of the Watt Scientific Library, founded by James Watt in 1816; to contain the books of the Greenock Library which was founded in 1783; to preserve the mathematical books which were formerly in the possession of the mathematician William Spence. It is now one of a number of libraries in the service which is organised by Inverclyde District Libraries.

Cathcart Square and Hamilton Street, Greenock.

106. CATHCART SQUARE AND HAMILTON STREET. The massive base of the Victoria Tower is seen in this view. The building to its left has been removed. This was formerly the premises of K. Irving, mantle and costume warehouse, who were located at Victoria Buildings, 2 Hamilton Street. This scene is now completely different as a result of the laying out of Clyde Square and the recently-constructed covered shopping precinct. On a historical note, there was a crater in the middle of Cathcart Square, where the Lyle Fountain now stands, as a result of the Greenock Blitz on 6th-7th May 1941. Similarly, enemy action at that time resulted in the removal of the roof on the entire front of the Municipal Buildings in Hamilton Street.

Greenock from the Whin Hill

VALENTINES SERIES

107. GREENOCK FROM THE WHIN HILL. The building on the left is the Merino Mill, which finally closed in 1981, having been in operation on this site since 1840. This panoramic view emphasises Greenock's geographical position on the Firth of Clyde. A number of vessels can be seen on the river. The town has a special claim to maritime fame, as it was from here that the first voyage was made across the Atlantic by a Greenock ship. This vessel was the 'George', which sailed in 1686 with a cargo and twenty-two prisoners who had been sentenced to transportation for life in Carolina for disaffection to the Government and for attending conventicles. On a further maritime note, Greenock was formerly a very important centre for the herring industry. In 1674 20,400 barrels of herring were exported to La Rochelle alone. Further quantities were exported to other parts of France and to Swedish and Baltic ports. The number of herring boats or 'busses' which belonged to Greenock and neighbouring towns in the late seventeenth century was over 300, about one half of which belonged to Greenock. The importance of this trade was indicated by the fact that the motto of the town at that time became the following: 'Let herrings swim that trade maintain.'

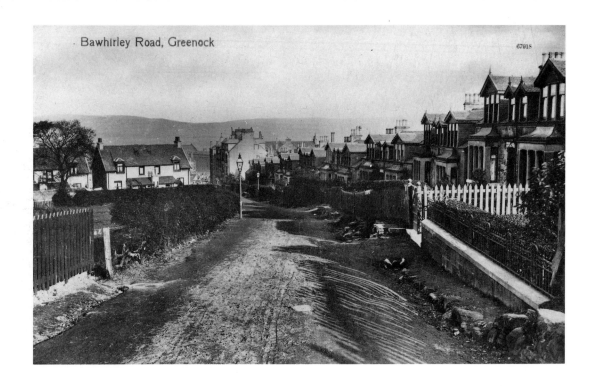

Bawhirley Road, Greenock

67918

108. BAWHIRLEY ROAD. This road has been re-surfaced and the condition of the pavement has been improved. Large lamp-standards have replaced the lamp-posts. The site to the immediate left is now occupied by the East Branch Library and new housing.